Even More TRUE STORIES

AN INTERMEDIATE READER

THIRD EDITION

by Sandra Heyer

PEARSON
Longman

In memory of my father, Edwin Heyer, who told his true stories of World War II

Even More True Stories, Third Edition

Pearson Education, 10 Bank Street, White Plains, NY 10606

Staff credits: The people who made up the **Even More True Stories, Third Edition** team, representing editorial, production, design, and manufacturing, are Danielle Belfiore, Elizabeth Carlson, Tracey Cataldo, Christine Edmonds, Nancy Flaggman, Laura Le Dréan, Françoise Leffler, Barbara Sabella, and Paula Van Ells.

Text composition and text art: Integra India Software Services
Text font: 10/14 New Aster
Illustrations: Don Martinetti
Maps: Burmar Technical Corporation
Text credits: See page 154.
Photo credits: See page 155.

Library of Congress Cataloging-in-Publication Data

Heyer, Sandra.
   Even more true stories/Sandra Heyer.—3rd ed.
   p.   cm.
   ISBN 0-13-175173-5 (student bk.: alk. paper)
   1. English language—Textbooks for foreign speakers. 2. Readers. I. Title.
   PE1128.H4356 2007
   428.6'4—dc22   2006026284

ISBN: 0-13-175173-5

Printed in the United States of America
6 7 8 9 10—V012—12 11

Contents

Introduction

Even More True Stories is an intermediate reader for students of English. It consists of 16 units centered around high-interest stories adapted from newspapers and magazines.

PRE-READING

A photograph introduces each unit. Pre-reading activities beneath it are suggested to motivate the students to read, to encourage predictions about the content of the reading, and to prompt students to share knowledge and experiences related to the topic.

If you have a mixed-level class or if your students need extra support, you might want to tell your students the story before they read it, stopping well short of the ending. As you tell the story, illustrate it with simple sketches on the board. (If you're not skilled at drawing—and many of us are not—please see the drawing tips in the To the Teacher section at the back of the book.) You could also write key vocabulary, including names and place names that might be unfamiliar, on the board; refer students to the map on page 153, which indicates the locations of the stories; or act out sections that lend themselves to dramatic interpretation. Some of the reading selections are expository—that is, their primary purpose is to transmit information— but even they begin with a story, and you can tell students those stories before they read. This pre-reading activity can be an enormously effective way to ease students into the intermediate level and is well worth the five or ten minutes you devote to it.

READING THE STORY

Some students might find it helpful to first skim the story by reading the first paragraph and the first sentences of subsequent paragraphs. Students who have a tendency to stop at each unfamiliar word should be encouraged to read silently twice: once without stopping, and then again, stopping to circle new vocabulary.

When all the students have finished reading, the teacher clarifies new vocabulary. If the students read at home, they use the vocabulary exercises to help clarify new words. If time permits, the teacher may wish to read the selection aloud while the students follow along in their texts. To engage students' interest as you read, invite them to "shadow read" with you—that is, to read silently but move their lips and tongues as if they were reading aloud.

Teachers might point out organizational devices used in the stories, such as introductory anecdotes, topic sentences, transitions, and conclusions.

THE EXERCISES

Each unit offers a variety of post-reading exercises. Students can work individually, in pairs, or in small groups. The exercises can be completed in class or assigned as homework. The answer key at the back of the book affords the teacher a choice in the method of correcting the exercises.

VOCABULARY

The vocabulary exercises are designed to aid comprehension by helping define unfamiliar words. The unfamiliar words in each story were identified by students who participated in field-testing the stories. The words that most students designated as "new" and that could be clearly explained were included in the exercises.

Research indicates that students' retention of new vocabulary depends not so much on the type of vocabulary exercises they complete but on how much exposure they have to the new words. The more times they "touch" a word, the more likely it is that they will remember it. So you will probably want to follow up the exercises in the text with supplemental activities, such as writing the words on flash cards and presenting them again in subsequent classes. Similarly, research shows that the particular method students use to learn vocabulary—whether they write the new words on small flash cards, for example, or in a vocabulary notebook—is not as important as simply having a system for memorizing vocabulary. For that reason, you might present several strategies for learning new words and encourage students to share their own techniques. Knowledge of vocabulary is a key component of reading comprehension, so it is important to devise a system for learning new words in class and to encourage students to devise their own systems for learning words at home.

COMPREHENSION/READING SKILLS

The comprehension exercises test students' understanding of the reading as well as introduce reading skills that will foster comprehension, such as scanning, making inferences, and forming mental images while reading.

Adult learners who do not have time to study English outside of class seem to appreciate having some class time set aside to complete the comprehension exercises on their own while you stand by ready to help. Reassure students that it is perfectly acceptable to refer back to the story to find the answers; it gives them practice with scanning.

DISCUSSION AND WRITING

Two spin-off exercises end each unit. A discussion exercise asks students to personalize the ideas and themes presented in the reading by discussing questions with classmates, sharing opinions, and exchanging information about their respective countries. Many of the discussion exercises require students first to complete an activity in pairs or small groups so that all students—even those in large classes—have a chance to participate. It is hoped that these discussions will provide further pleasure from the reading process and give insights into cultural similarities and differences.

The final exercise is a guided writing based on the reading. The examples are the work of intermediate-level ESL students.

CHALLENGE PAGES

The Challenge pages are intended to do what the title suggests: provide a challenging reading experience for students who are ready for more difficult material. The level of difficulty is a half-step up from that in the main story. The main stories were written with an audience of intermediate-level ESL students in mind; vocabulary and sentence structure were controlled. The Challenge pages, however, were written for an audience whose native language is English, with no special consideration given to vocabulary or sentence structure. The intent of these pages is to facilitate the transition from controlled to authentic written English. Students who participated in field-testing the Challenge pages seemed to take pride in knowing they were reading "real English," not English written specifically for the ESL student.

The stories, the exercises, and the Challenge pages are intended to build students' confidence along with their reading skills. Above all, it is hoped that reading *Even More True Stories* will be a pleasure, for both you and your students.

UNIT

1

1. PRE-READING

Think about these questions. Discuss your answers with your classmates.

▶ Look at the title of the story. What does *love at first sight* mean?

▶ Do you believe people can fall in love "at first sight"?

▶ Do you know anyone who fell in love at first sight? Tell the class the story.

Love at First Sight

When Pamela Claypole was 56 years old, her whole life changed. She was outside working in her garden on a Saturday morning when suddenly she felt dizzy. That's all she remembers. Neighbors found her lying on the ground, unconscious. At a nearby hospital, doctors made their diagnosis: Pamela had had a stroke. She couldn't move the left side of her body, and she couldn't see, hear, or speak. Gradually, she got better. In a few months, she was able to use the left side of her body again, and she was able to hear and speak. But she still couldn't see. Her doctors told her she might be blind for the rest of her life.

Pamela came home from the hospital and began learning to live without her sight. It wasn't easy. Pamela was single, and she lived alone. There were days when she wished she hadn't survived the stroke. But as time went on, she began to adjust. She learned to take care of herself—to cook, to clean, to shop. There were just a few things she couldn't do. She couldn't fix things in her house, for example. When something broke, her friends had to help her.

One morning about three years after her stroke, Pamela was washing dishes and realized that the water wasn't going down the drain in her kitchen sink. It was probably clogged. "Call Mitch," her friends told her. Mitch was the local handyman. He fixed things for people and helped them with jobs around the house. He was middle-aged and single, and he loved his work.

Pamela called Mitch. "I hear you're a pretty good plumber," she said. "I've got a problem with my kitchen sink. Can you come over?"

"I'll be right there," Mitch told her. He fixed the sink in just a few minutes. "All done," he said.

"Thank you. How much do I owe you?" Pamela asked.

"Nothing," Mitch said. "But a cup of tea would be nice."

Pamela made some tea, and she and Mitch sat at her kitchen table and talked. He told her he would be happy to help her anytime.

Over the next two years, Mitch came to Pamela's house often to fix something or to work with her in the garden. He never accepted a penny from Pamela for the work he did; he said a cup of tea and a little conversation were payment enough. The truth was that Mitch was in love with Pamela. He never told her, though. Mitch was not a handsome man. "If she could see me," he thought, "she wouldn't love me."

One morning Pamela woke up early. She turned her head on the pillow and saw the hands on the alarm clock next to her bed: 5:30 A.M. She could see! She ran to the front door of her house and looked outside. She could see the flowers, the trees, the houses across the street. She cried with happiness. Then she went to the phone and called her best friend, Mitch.

"Hello, Mitch," she said. "It's an emergency! Come quick!"

Mitch thought about Pamela's phone call as he threw on some clothes. What kind of emergency could there be at 5:30 in the morning? Was there water everywhere? Was someone trying to break into her house? He ran the half mile to Pamela's house.

Pamela opened the front door. "Pam, are you okay?" Mitch said. Pamela looked at him and smiled. "Your eyes are brown," she said.

"What?" he asked.

"Your eyes are brown," she repeated.

"You can see?"

"Yes!" Pamela said and threw her arms around Mitch. Mitch was happy for Pamela, and he was also happy for himself. "She can see me, and she still likes me," he thought.

A few weeks later, Mitch asked Pamela to marry him, and she said yes. He told her that he had loved her from the first moment he saw her, when he came to fix her sink.

"Why didn't you ever tell me?" Pamela asked him.

"I thought you wouldn't want me because I'm not handsome," Mitch said.

"I don't care what you look like," Pamela told Mitch. "I've loved you for years."

"Well, why didn't you tell me?" he asked.

"I thought you wouldn't want me," she answered, "because I was blind."

2. VOCABULARY

◆ LOOKING AT THE STORY

Complete the sentences with the words in the box. Write the correct words on the lines.

accepted	dizzy	nearby	stroke
adjust	handyman	owe	threw on some clothes
clogged	might	sight	unconscious
come over			

1. Pamela was working in her garden when suddenly it seemed that everything was going around and around. She felt _____*dizzy*_____.

2. When neighbors found Pamela, her eyes were closed and she was lying on the ground. They couldn't wake her up. She was _____.

3. Neighbors took Pamela to a _____ hospital. It was only a mile from her house.

4. Pamela couldn't move the left side of her body, and she couldn't hear, speak, or see. She had had a _____.

5. Pamela asked her doctors, "Will I see again?" They said, "We're not sure." They told her she _____ be blind for the rest of her life.

6. When Pamela came home from the hospital, she couldn't see. It was difficult to live without her _____.

7. Pamela had to change the ways she did things. She had to learn new ways of cleaning, cooking, and shopping. She had to _____ to being blind.

8. Mitch fixed things for people and helped them with small jobs around the house. He was a _____.

9. Pamela wanted Mitch to come to her house to fix the sink. So she called him and asked, "Can you _____?"

10. The water wasn't going down in the sink because there was something in the drain. The drain was _____.

11. Pamela wanted to know the cost after Mitch fixed her sink. "How much do I
_____ you?" she asked.

12. Mitch didn't take any money for his work. He never _____ a penny.

13. Pamela called Mitch and said, "Come quick! It's an emergency!" Mitch didn't take
time to dress carefully. He just _____ and ran to Pamela's house.

◆ **LOOKING AT A NEW CONTEXT**

**Read these sentences. If the sentence is true for you, circle *Yes*. If it is not true for you,
circle *No*. Explain your *Yes* answers. Write your explanations on the lines. Then share
your *Yes* answers in a small group. Here, for example, is what one student wrote about
a *Yes* sentence.**

Someone owes me money.   (YES)   NO

My brother owes me $200.
_____

1. I have been unconscious.   YES   NO
_____

2. I need a handyman to do some work in my home.   YES   NO
_____

3. I know someone who had a stroke.   YES   NO
_____

4. Sometimes I just throw on some clothes and don't
take time to dress carefully.   YES   NO
_____

5. This year I had to adjust to something new.   YES   NO
_____

6. I owe someone some money.   YES   NO
_____

7. Someone owes me money.   YES   NO
_____

8. A lot of my relatives live nearby.   YES   NO
_____

3. COMPREHENSION/READING SKILLS

◆ FORMING MENTAL IMAGES AS YOU READ

Do you see pictures in your mind as you read? Look at these pictures. Find the sentence in the story that goes with each picture. Copy the sentence on the lines.

1. *Neighbors found her lying on the ground, unconscious.*

2. _____

_____

3. _____

_____

4. _____

_____

5. _____

6. _____

7. _____

8. _____

9. _____

◆ UNDERSTANDING CAUSE AND EFFECT

Find the best way to complete each sentence. Write the letter of your answer on the line.

_____ 1. Pamela fell to the ground

_____ 2. It was not easy for Pamela to adjust to being blind

_____ 3. Pamela called Mitch

_____ 4. Mitch thought Pamela wouldn't love him

_____ 5. Pamela thought Mitch wouldn't love her

a. because she was single and lived alone.

b. because he wasn't handsome.

c. because she had had a stroke.

d. because she was blind.

e. because the drain in her sink was clogged.

4. DISCUSSION

Mitch thought Pamela wouldn't love him because he wasn't handsome. How important is it to be handsome or beautiful?

Discuss the importance of a person's physical appearance.

1. Work as a class to make a list of qualities that are important when you are looking for a husband, wife, boyfriend, or girlfriend. Your teacher will write your list on the board. For example:

   handsome / pretty
   honest
   hardworking

From the qualities on the board, choose two that are very important to you and two that are not important. Write those qualities in the chart below. Then compare your answers with a classmate's.

Very Important	Not Important
_____	_____
_____	_____

2. Form two groups: men in one group and women in another. The men and women will go to different parts of the room, or one group will go to a different room. The women will make a list of the four qualities they think are most important when choosing a husband, and the men will make a list of the four qualities they think are most important when choosing a wife. Then the two groups will come back together. Did the men and women choose the same qualities?

3. How important is physical appearance in the United States? In small groups, read the following statements. Circle *T* if you think the statement is true and *F* if you think the statement is false. Your group must decide on only one answer for each statement. Report your group's answers to the whole class. Then look in the Answer Key to see if you guessed correctly.

   a. In political elections, the more handsome man usually wins.   T   F

   b. In presidential elections, the taller man usually wins.   T   F

   c. Tall people make more money than short people.   T   F

   d. Attractive people make more money than unattractive people.   T   F

   e. Teachers think attractive students are smarter than   T   F
      unattractive students.

f. People usually marry people who are as attractive as they are.   T   F

g. Babies look at the faces of attractive people longer than they   T   F
look at the faces of unattractive people.

h. Attractive people who have a problem get more help than   T   F
unattractive people.

5. WRITING

After Mitch fixed Pamela's sink, Pamela made some tea and they sat at her kitchen table and talked. What do men and women talk about when they're getting to know each other? What do you think Pamela and Mitch talked about?

A. Work as a class to make three lists.

1. Topics that men talk about when they are with other men

2. Topics women talk about when they are with other women

3. Topics for a man and woman to talk about when they are together

Your teacher will write your lists on the board.

B. Choose one of the following writing activities.

1. With a partner, write out a conversation between a man and woman when they first meet. The woman should speak six to eight times, and the man should speak six to eight times. Practice the conversation with your partner. If you would like to, read it in front of the class. One person plays the part of the woman, and the other person plays the part of the man.

2. With a partner, write out Pamela and Mitch's first conversation. Pamela should speak six to eight times, and Mitch should speak six to eight times. Practice the conversation with your partner. If you would like to, read it in front of the class. One person plays the part of Pamela, and the other person plays the part of Mitch.

Robert Fulghum is the author of a book called *True Love*. The book is a collection of true love stories that ordinary people told him. How did he collect these stories? He sat in coffee houses in Seattle next to a sign that said, "TELL ME A SHORT LOVE STORY AND I WILL BUY YOU COFFEE AND MAKE YOU FAMOUS." The sign always drew a crowd. Once a crowd gathered, Fulghum encouraged people to tell their love stories. He wrote down the best stories and published them in the book. Here are two love stories from Fulghum's book. He says these stories are even better when read aloud to someone you love.

Read the love stories.

◆ Flowers

You wanted really short love stories. This one's long but small. I go to the Pike Place Market in Seattle almost every Saturday morning to shop and carry on a love affair.

For several years, I've bought flowers from a youngish woman who is a refugee from one of the hill tribes of Indochina. For one thing, she has the freshest and most beautiful flowers. For another, she is a fresh and beautiful flower herself. I don't know her name, nor she mine. We don't speak the same language. To her, I must be just another customer.

She is spring to me. She's there with daffodils, pussy willows, and then irises. She's summer, with roses and sunflowers. She's fall, with dahlias and chrysanthemums. As the growing season comes to an end, she brings stems of fall leaves to sell, and then it's over. In winter, I miss her.

When we exchange flowers and money, I always try to briefly and slyly touch her hand.

I always insist she keep the change, and she always insists on giving me an extra flower.

Once I tried to buy all her flowers at once, but she just shook her head no. I don't know why. Maybe she, too, is in love with someone and wants to be there to sell him flowers when he comes.

◆ Peanuts

This is really my mother's love story. I asked her to tell you, but she's too shy. It's too good not to pass on. It explains why my brother and I say we owe our existence to peanuts.

When she graduated from high school, my mother had everything going for her but one. She was pretty, smart, and came from a well-to-do family, but she was terribly shy—

especially around men. Boys didn't like to take her out because she was so quiet. She went off to the same college her mother had gone to, and, to please her mother, she agreed to join her mother's sorority. At the first sorority party, she sat out of sight at one end of a room in a corner by a table that had snacks on it. She ate a lot of peanuts out of nervousness.

She began to notice a waiter, who seemed to be as shy as she. He never said anything, but he was taking care of her. He kept her glass filled with nonalcoholic punch and kept her peanut bowl full. From time to time, their eyes met and they smiled at each other.

When the dancing started and the party got rowdy, she walked into the kitchen and out the back door to escape. As she was going down the alley, she heard someone calling, "Wait, wait, please wait." It was the waiter, running down the alley after her with a paper bag in his hands. They stood in awkward silence, just smiling. Then he reached into the bag, pulled out a whole can of peanuts and offered them to her and said, "I only wish these were pearls."

He ran back up the alley and into the sorority house.

Well, one thing led to another.

Twenty-five years later, on the silver wedding anniversary of my mother and the waiter (my father), he gave her a sterling silver jar marked "peanuts." She thought that was the gift and was really pleased. But there was more. When she lifted the lid, inside was a string of pearls.

No gift ever pleased her more. She wore those pearls as her only jewelry for years. When my father was killed in a traffic accident, she put the silver peanut can in his coffin with him. I've never seen her wear the pearls since. I think I know where they are, but I'm too shy to ask.

Choose one of the following writing activities.

Imagine that the flower seller in the story "Flowers" speaks a little English. With a partner, write out a conversation between the flower seller and the customer. The flower seller should speak six to eight times, and the customer should speak six to eight times. Practice the conversation with your partner. If you would like, read it in front of the class. One person plays the part of the flower seller, and the other person plays the part of the customer.

In the story "Peanuts," the waiter runs after the young woman and gives her a can of peanuts. He says, "I only wish these were pearls." With a partner, continue the conversation between the waiter and the young woman. Write six to eight lines for each one. Practice the conversation with your partner. If you would like, read it in front of the class. One person plays the part of the waiter, and the other person plays the part of the young woman.

UNIT 2

1. PRE-READING

What do you know about the tsunami of 2004? Share what you know with the class. Your teacher will write the information on the board and organize it in an idea map. For example, one class began their idea map this way:

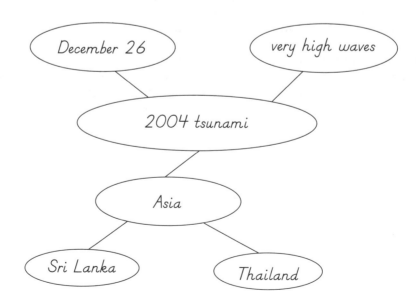

The Semong (The Tsunami)

On the island of Simeulue in Indonesia, an old woman was telling a story to her grandchildren. "Once upon a time," she began, "there was a little girl named Kiro. Kiro lived in our village a long time ago—before you were born, before your parents were born, even before I was born. One day Kiro was in her house, helping her mother in the kitchen. Suddenly the ground began to shake. It shook and shook. It shook so hard that Kiro and her mother couldn't stand up, and they fell to the floor. All around them, dishes and pots were falling from the shelves and crashing to the floor. Finally, the shaking stopped. Kiro and her mother got up and walked out of their house."

"Then what happened, Grandma?" the children asked, although they knew what happened next. They had heard the story many times before.

"Kiro looked toward the beach," the grandmother continued, "and she saw something she had never seen before. All the water was leaving the beach. It was going out toward the sea. Where there once had been a narrow beach, there was a wide beach. Beautiful, colorful fish were lying all over the beach. Some people were picking up the fish and putting them in baskets. Other people were standing on the beach looking out at the water. But Kiro remembered the story her grandmother had told her. So she yelled to the people."

Here the grandmother paused. "Do you remember what Kiro yelled?" she asked her grandchildren.

"Run!" the children answered.

"That's right. Kiro yelled, 'Run! *Semong*!' Do you remember what a *semong* is?"

"A big wave!" the children answered.

"Yes," the old woman said. "A very big wave. Bigger than a boy. Bigger than a girl. Bigger than a house. Bigger than a palm tree."

She continued the story.

" 'Run! *Semong*!' Kiro yelled. People put down their baskets of fish. They picked up their children. They ran to the hills behind our village. Then the *semong* came. A wall of water came toward the village. The water covered the beach and covered the houses and covered the trees. But all the people were safe because they were standing on the hills. And that is the story of Kiro and the *semong*."

Why was the old woman telling her grandchildren this story? She was warning them. In 1907, a tsunami—a giant wave—had hit their island, and many people had died. She wanted the children to be ready if another tsunami came.

Another tsunami did come to Simeulue. On the morning of December 26, 2004, an earthquake in the Indian Ocean created huge waves. The waves came first to Simeulue, the island closest to the earthquake.

A 33-year-old man named Suhardin, who lives on the coast of Simeulue, told a reporter about his experience. He said his grandmother had told him stories about the *semong*. But he didn't think about his grandmother's stories when he felt the earthquake. Nothing had happened after an earthquake three years ago. Why would there be a *semong* after this earthquake? But then a man ran past him yelling, "*Semong*! *Semong*!" Suhardin thought about his grandmother and decided to climb one of the hills behind his village.

When he got to the top of the hill, hundreds of people were already there, and more people were climbing the steep hill. Some were helping old people up the hill, and some were carrying small children. Before long, everyone in the village was on top of the hill, looking out toward the sea. For thirty minutes, nothing happened. Then, just as Suhardin was thinking about walking back down the hill, the water along the coast rushed out to the sea. After that, the first wave came: A wall of water 10 meters high crashed on the shore below. Suhardin watched the water take his whole village out to sea.

The tsunami of 2004 hit fourteen countries, and more than 280,000 people died. But on the island of Simeulue, with 75,000 people, only 7 died. Why did so many people on Simeulue survive?

(continued)

They survived for two reasons. First, they survived because Simeulue's hills are close to the coast. When the tsunami came, people could run to safety. People in other places were not so lucky; they had no nearby hills to run to. Second, they survived because they remembered the stories the old people told about the *semong*, stories that warned them to run to the hills after an earthquake.

The people of Simeulue hope another tsunami never comes to their island. But just in case, they will tell their grandchildren the story of the *semong*. Someday the story could save their grandchildren's lives, just as the story saved theirs.

2. VOCABULARY

♦ **LOOKING AT THE STORY**

Complete the sentences with the words in the box. Write the correct words on the lines.

coast	island	survived	whole
crashed	paused	village	wide
huge	steep	warn	yelled

1. There is water all around Simeulue. It is an _____ *island* _____.

2. Only 500 people lived in Kiro's _____.

3. The dishes and pots made a loud noise when they _____ to the floor.

4. The beach near Kiro's village was narrow, but after the water left, it was

   _____.

5. Kiro's grandmother stopped in her story because she wanted to be sure the children understood the word *semong*. She _____ for a minute and asked them, "Do you remember what a *semong* is?"

6. Everyone on the beach heard Kiro because she spoke loudly. "Run!" she

   _____.

7. The grandmother wanted the children to be ready if another dangerous tsunami came. She wanted to _____ them.

8. The first wave was over 10 meters high. It was _____.

9. Suhardin didn't live in the center of the island; he lived close to the water, on the

   _____.

10. It was difficult for old people and children to climb the hill behind Suhardin's village because the hill was _____.

11. The water covered everything in Suhardin's village—houses and shops, bicycles and cars. The water took the _____ village out to sea.

12. Simeulue had 75,000 people. Seven people died, and 74,993 _____.

◆ LOOKING AT A NEW CONTEXT

A. Choose five words from the list of words on page 14 that you want to remember. Use each word in your own sentence. Write your sentences on the lines below. Here, for example, is a sentence one student wrote using the word *huge*.

I saw a huge bear at the zoo. _____

1. _____

2. _____

3. _____

4. _____

5. _____

If you would like to test your memory of the new words, try this: Cross out the five words so that you can't read them. For example:

I saw a ~~huge~~ bear at the zoo. _____

When you are finished with the exercises in this unit, come back to this exercise. Can you remember the words you crossed out?

B. Sometimes you can write a word in a way that helps you remember it. For example, you can write the word *wide* this way:

$$W \quad I \quad D \quad E$$

Think about these words from the story: *crash, huge, island, pause, steep*. Choose one of the words. In the space below, write it in a way that helps you remember it. If you would like to, write the word on the board and share your idea with the class.

3. COMPREHENSION/READING SKILLS

◆ **UNDERSTANDING THE MAIN IDEA**

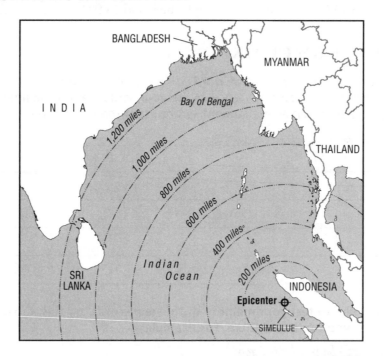

Imagine this: You and a friend are looking at the map above. It shows the countries and islands that the 2004 tsunami hit.

Your friend points to the island of Simeulue. "The tsunami must have caused a lot of damage there," your friend says.

"It did," you answer. "But almost everyone on the island survived."

"Really?" your friend says. "Why was that?"

Explain to your friend why almost everyone on Simeulue survived. Write your explanation on the lines.

_____

_____

_____

_____

_____

_____

Look at the story for answers to the questions below. Write your answers on the lines. Work quickly; try to complete this exercise in three minutes or less.

1. What country does the island of Simeulue belong to? _____

2. What was the name of the little girl in the story? _____

3. In what year did a tsunami kill many people on Simeulue? _____

4. What was the month and day of the 2004 earthquake in the Indian Ocean?

   _____

5. How old is Suhardin? _____

6. Where does he live on Simeulue? _____

7. How long did Suhardin stand on top of the hill before the tsunami came?

   _____

8. How high was the first wave that hit Simeulue? _____

9. How many countries did the 2004 tsunami hit? _____

10. How many people live on Simeulue? _____

4. DISCUSSION

A tsunami is a natural disaster. Talk about natural disasters that happen in your native country and in your classmates' native countries. Follow the steps below.

1. Work as a class to make a list of natural disasters (for example, tsunamis, hurricanes). Your teacher will write your list on the board.

2. Copy the words in the spaces along the top of the chart on the next page.

3. On the left side of the chart, write the names of your classmates' countries.

4. Walk around the room and find a person from each country. Ask your classmates if the natural disasters written at the top of the chart happen in their countries. (For example, ask, "Do you have hurricanes in Korea?")

5. Check (✓) your classmates' "yes" answers.

6. Ask your classmates for more information about their "yes" answers.

(continued)

Country	tsunami							

5. WRITING

A. The old woman told a story to warn her grandchildren about a tsunami. All over the world, people tell stories that warn of danger or teach a lesson.

Write a story that warns of danger or teaches a lesson. It can be a story that people in your country tell, a story from your personal life, or a story that you made up. Here is what one student wrote.

When I lived in California, there were earthquakes sometimes. One day when there was an earthquake, my friend was at home with her baby. She ran to the baby's bed, picked up the baby, and ran to a doorway. She stood in the doorway and held the baby. A piece of the ceiling fell down on the baby's bed. So if there is an earthquake, stand in a doorway.

B. Have you ever experienced a natural disaster? Write about your experience. Here is what one student wrote.

Costa Rica is a small country, but it has eight volcanoes. Currently three of them are active, so we have many earthquakes.

I remember one (among many), on December 22, 1990, in my city, San José. My brother Eduardo was visiting us then. We lived in a second-floor apartment with wood floors. Eduardo is a big man, and when he walked across the floor, the floor made a noise. I told him three times, "Eduardo, don't make so much noise when you walk. It bothers the people living below us." He told me, "I'm not making noise." Then we realized an earthquake was causing the floor to make noise. A few minutes later, we had an earthquake of 6.2 on the Richter scale.

When the earthquake was over, my brother said, "Let's go see the damage the earthquake did." I told him, "Eduardo, let's not go because we might have another earthquake." But he insisted, so we went. We walked through San José's avenues. There were many signs and cables on the ground. The walls of some buildings had fallen down. A man told us that he had been ready to get into his car when the earthquake happened and the wall of a building fell down on it.

Days later, friends told me that they had been in a supermarket and could hear glass breaking as jars of food crashed to the floor.

Fortunately nobody died in that earthquake, but there was a lot of damage.

Many popular vacation spots are in the area hit by the 2004 tsunami, so some of the people who experienced it were tourists. Following are three stories of people who were on vacation when the tsunami hit. They are first-person accounts; that is, the people told the stories in their own words.

Read each story. Then complete the exercises following the stories.

Name: Jillian Searle
Home country: Australia
Age: 32
Occupation: Homemaker

My husband and I were on vacation in Phuket, Thailand,[1] with our two sons: Lachie, who's 5, and Blake, who's 2. We were all relaxing at the hotel pool. My husband had just left—he'd gone back up to our room to get some clothes for Blake. I saw a big wall of water coming straight for us, and I just started running. I had both my boys in my arms, one in each arm, and we started going under. I knew that if I held on to both, we would all die. I just thought I'd better let go of Lachie, the oldest. He was squeezing me and saying, "Don't let go of me, Mummy." I saw a teenage girl nearby. "Grab him!" I screamed to her as I let go of Lachie's hand. She grabbed hold of him for a moment, but she had to let go because she was going under. And then I couldn't see Lachie.

After the water receded, my husband and I looked for Lachie. I was screaming trying to find him. We thought he was dead. I remember telling my husband, "There is no way I can live my life knowing that I took his hand off mine." We looked for about two hours, and then we found him with a hotel security guard. He'd kept his head above water by holding onto a door in the hotel lobby.

We are so lucky. I'm just thankful I still have my two kids with me.

Name: Stephen Boulton
Home country: Scotland
Age: 34
Occupation: Plumber and volunteer firefighter

I was celebrating my 34th birthday with my wife and three children—they're 12, 4, and 2—at a resort in the Maldives.[2] We were on the pier when suddenly the tide came in. Before we knew

it, the water was up to our chests. It was so strong that we knew if we fell, it would pull us under. My wife and I grabbed our kids and waded through horrendous currents back to our hotel. When we turned around to look at the pier, we saw that it was gone.

After about five minutes, the tide went back out as far as you could see, as if someone pulled the plug. I didn't like what I was seeing. We climbed up a palm tree with the younger kids on our backs. I tied each child to a branch of the tree with beach towels. Then the second wave came. It was like the whole sea was heading our way. It sped past within inches of our feet. After the water receded, I climbed down to help the injured, but my family stayed up in the tree for a couple of hours, just to be on the safe side.

I never thought for a second we wouldn't be OK. From the moment it all started going crazy, I worked out every possible scenario—and solutions. That's just the way I am.

Name: Tilly Smith
Home country: England
Age: 10
Occupation: Student

I was on holiday with my parents and little sister in Phuket, Thailand. We were on the beach, and the water started to go funny. There were bubbles, and then the tide went out all of a sudden. I recognized what was happening and had a feeling there was going to be a tsunami. Just two weeks before, our geography teacher had taught us about earthquakes and how they cause tsunamis. He told us that after the sea sucked backwards, a tsunami would come in five or ten minutes. When the water went back, I said, "Mummy, we must get off the beach *now*." My mum wanted to look at what was going on, but when I told her about tsunamis, she had second thoughts. We ran off the beach as fast as we could. My parents warned the other people on the beach—there were about 100 people there—and they all ran, too. We went up to the third floor of our hotel. A few minutes later, the tsunami came. After the wave came, I said to Mummy, "I told you."

[1] Phuket Island is off the west coast of Thailand. It is 500 kilometers from the epicenter of the earthquake.

[2] The Republic of Maldives is an island nation southwest of India. It consists of 1,192 islands, 200 of which are inhabited. It is 2,252 kilometers west of the epicenter of the earthquake.

A. Look at the following photos. Which photo goes with which story? Write the number of the story on the line below the photo.

a. _____

b. _____

c. _____

B. Read the newspaper headlines below. Which headline goes with which story? Write the number of the story next to the correct headline.

_____ Family saved by their towels

_____ Geography lesson saves family

_____ Which child to save?

UNIT 3

1. PRE-READING

Compare gestures in your native country with gestures in other countries. Your teacher will ask you the questions below. Answer the questions using only your hands, arms, and head. Don't speak! As you answer each question, look at your classmates. Which gestures are the same? Which gestures are different?

What gesture do you use for . . . ?

1. Come here.
2. Go away.
3. Stop.
4. Please be quiet.
5. I can't hear you.
6. You have a phone call.
7. Who, me?
8. Yes.
9. No.
10. I don't know.
11. Wait a minute.
12. He/She's crazy.
13. He/She's intelligent.
14. Money
15. A long time ago
16. This is good.
17. This is bad.
18. This is delicious.

More Alike Than Different

Everyone listened attentively as the woman spoke.

"If you want to say 'OK,' don't make a circle with your thumb and first finger," the woman began. "That means OK here in the United States, but in Russia it's an obscene gesture."

The audience of 300 Americans chuckled; a few people took notes.

"It's all right to admire something," the woman continued, "but don't be too enthusiastic. Don't say, 'I *really* like your tablecloth.' Your Russian friend will offer you the tablecloth and will be offended if you don't take it.

"Remember that, in general, life in Russia is not as comfortable as life in the United States. You might not have hot running water, or you might have to share a bathroom with five or six people."

The woman was preparing the Americans for their trip to Russia. In Russia, the language, customs, and food would be different. Even simple things, like making a phone call, would be different. The Americans wanted to learn about these differences before their trip. They didn't want to experience culture shock.

When they arrived in Russia, the Americans were glad that they had prepared for their trip. Most of them experienced only a little culture shock. They enjoyed their visit and made a lot of Russian friends.

Making friends was, in fact, the purpose of the trip. It was planned by Friendship Force International, an organization that promotes world peace. Friendship Force International believes that people who are friends will not fight wars. So, to help people from all over the world become friends, it organizes exchanges of people. It has sent more than a half million people to live with families in other countries for a week or two. The U.S.-Russian exchange was one of the largest exchanges it has ever organized. Friendship Force sent 300 Americans to Russia and 300 Russians to the United States.

The Russians, like the Americans, prepared for their visit by learning about life in the other country. Still, they too experienced a little culture shock.

The Russians knew that Americans were fond of pets, but they were shocked to see pets inside homes. They couldn't believe their eyes when they saw dogs eating in the kitchen and sleeping on people's beds.

They were surprised at the differences between everyday life in Russia and in the United States. The Americans' lives, they said, were much easier. A Russian woman gasped when she saw an American pour rice directly from a box into a pan of boiling water. "You didn't wash the rice?" she asked. She explained that at home she had to wash the rice carefully and pick out all the stones. "Are you kidding?" the American said. "If people here had to do that, nobody would buy rice."

The Russians knew that Americans liked to eat fast food in restaurants, but they were disappointed to see that Americans ate fast meals at home, too. In Russia, the evening meal often lasts an hour or two because families sit at the table and talk. When American families eat together—*if* they eat together—they often eat quickly and don't take time for long conversations. The Russians thought that was a shame.

In spite of their differences in language and culture, the Russians and Americans became friends. In fact, most people who go on Friendship Force trips make friends, no matter where they go. The women in the photo, for example, became friends during a Friendship Force exchange in Vietnam. The woman with the light-colored hair is from the United States. For two weeks, she was the guest of a Vietnamese woman and her two daughters. By the end of the visit, the four women were friends, even though not long ago their countries were enemies.

Perhaps an 11-year-old girl summarized the Friendship Force experience best. She and some children from her school traveled to Russia with the American group. When they returned to the United States, their teacher asked them to write about their trip. She wrote, "I have learned a lot from this experience. I learned to adapt to a different culture. And I learned that people all over the world are more alike than they are different."

2. VOCABULARY

◆ LOOKING AT THE STORY

Read the following sentences. Then complete the statements about the words in italics. Circle the letter of the correct answer.

▶ Everyone listened *attentively* as the woman spoke.

  1. To listen attentively is to listen _____.
    (a.) carefully   b. nervously

▶ "Don't make a circle with your thumb and first finger," the woman said. "That's an *obscene* gesture in Russia." *The audience* of 300 Americans *chuckled*.

  2. An obscene gesture is _____.
    a. not polite   b. polite

  3. An audience _____.
    a. listens or watches   b. sings, dances, or speaks

  4. To chuckle is to _____.
    a. sing loudly   b. laugh quietly

▶ "It's all right to *admire* something," the woman said, "but don't be too *enthusiastic*. Don't say, 'I really like your tablecloth.' Your Russian friend will offer you the tablecloth and will be *offended* if you don't take it."

  5. If you admire something, you _____.
    a. don't like it   b. like it

  6. If you are enthusiastic, you are _____.
    a. interested and excited   b. bored and tired

  7. People who are offended are _____.
    a. a little angry because their   b. a little nervous because they
       feelings are hurt   don't know what to do

▶ The Russians knew that Americans were *fond of* pets.

  8. People who are fond of pets _____.
    a. don't like pets   b. like pets

▶ A Russian woman *gasped* when she saw an American pour rice directly from a box into a pan of boiling water. "You didn't wash the rice?" she asked.

  9. People gasp when they are _____.
    a. tired   b. surprised

▶ The Russians knew that Americans liked to eat fast food in restaurants, but they were *disappointed* to see that Americans ate fast meals at home, too.

  10. People who are disappointed are _____.
    a. not happy   b. happy

▶ An 11-year-old girl wrote, "I learned to *adapt* to a new culture. And I learned that people all over the world are more *alike* than they are different."

11. People who adapt _____.
    a. don't change   b. change

12. *Alike* means _____.
    a. the same   b. strange

◆ LOOKING AT A NEW CONTEXT

Complete the sentences to show that you understand the meanings of the new words. Then in small groups, take turns reading your sentences aloud. Ask your classmates questions about their sentences.

1. Someone I really admire is _____.

2. Someone or something that makes me chuckle is _____.

3. People who immigrate to the United States probably find it difficult to adapt to

   _____.

4. People who immigrate to the United States probably find it easy to adapt to

   _____.

5. I would listen attentively if someone were talking about _____.

6. I would be disappointed if someone gave me _____ for my birthday.

7. I would be enthusiastic if someone invited me to _____.

8. I would gasp with surprise if I heard that _____.

3. COMPREHENSION/READING SKILLS

◆ UNDERSTANDING THE MAIN IDEAS

Circle the letter of the best answer.

1. "More Alike Than Different" is about _____.
   a. the language, customs, and food in Russia
   b. a U.S.-Russian exchange of people that was organized by Friendship Force International
   c. communicating through sign language and dictionaries

2. Friendship Force International is _____.
   a. an international organization that promotes world peace
   b. an organization that prepares Americans for visiting Russia
   c. an international organization of children who visit other countries

(continued)

3. Friendship Force International believes that _____.
   a. people who live in Russia don't have comfortable lives
   b. people who are friends won't fight wars
   c. people who don't speak English will experience culture shock in the United States

4. To help people become friends, Friendship Force International _____.
   a. sends language teachers all over the world
   b. mails letters all over the world
   c. organizes exchanges of people

5. The Americans prepared for their visit by _____.
   a. experiencing culture shock
   b. writing essays
   c. learning about Russian life

6. Although their languages and cultures were different, the Russians and the Americans _____.
   a. ate the same food
   b. became friends
   c. had the same everyday lives

◆ **UNDERSTANDING SUPPORTING DETAILS**

Find the best way to complete each sentence. Write the letter of your answer on the line.

_____ 1. "It's all right to admire something, but don't be too enthusiastic. For example,

_____ 2. Friendship Force International organizes exchanges of people. For example,

_____ 3. The Russians were shocked to see pets inside homes. For example,

_____ 4. The Russians said that the Americans' lives were much easier than theirs. For example,

_____ 5. Most people who go on Friendship Force trips make friends. For example,

a. they couldn't believe their eyes when they saw dogs eating in the kitchen.

b. the four women in the photo became friends, even though not long ago their countries were enemies.

c. don't say, 'I *really* like your tablecloth.' "

d. Russians have to wash their rice carefully, but Americans don't.

e. the organization sent 300 Americans to Russia and 300 Russians to the United States.

4. DISCUSSION

A. Are you and your classmates more alike than different? Find out. Sit in groups of three. Continue asking one another questions until you discover three things you have in common. (For example: "We all like cats. We all have birthdays in August.") Then report back to the class.

B. When people move to a new country, they often go through three stages. These are the stages:

Stage 1: Arrival
▶ Everything is new and different
▶ Happy, excited

Stage 3: One to two years after arrival
▶ Can speak new language, understand customs, laugh at mistakes
▶ Adapted, feel "at home"

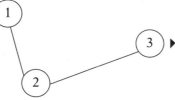

Stage 2: Six weeks to six months after arrival
▶ Everything in native country seems better
▶ Sad, want to go home

Are you in a new country? If so, where are you—at Stage 1, Stage 2, Stage 3, or somewhere in between? Put an X to show where you are. Then show a classmate where you put your X. Tell your classmate why you put your X where you did.

5. WRITING

A. Imagine that Friendship Force International is sending a group of people to your native country. What might surprise the visitors? Write a paragraph to prepare the visitors so that they don't experience culture shock. Here is what one student wrote.

> Be careful when you shop in Syria. The prices you see in store windows are sometimes not the actual prices. For example, you might see a pair of shoes in a store window. Next to the shoes is the price. But when you go into the store, you find out that the real price of the shoes is more than the price in the window. So, Syrians don't always believe the prices they see in store windows. If people from other countries believe those prices, they will have a bad surprise.

B. Are you living in another country? Imagine that friends or relatives from your country are coming to visit. What might surprise them? Write them a letter. Prepare them so that they don't experience culture shock.

CHALLENGE

Test your knowledge of other cultures and customs. Imagine this: You are traveling around the world and you find yourself in the following situations.

Read about each situation. Then answer the question, circling the letter of the best answer. (The answers—and explanations of the answers—are in the Answer Key.)

You are visiting a temple in Thailand. In the courtyard of the temple, people are sitting on the ground. They are resting and talking. You are tired, so you sit down on the ground, too. You lean back on the temple wall and stretch your feet out in front of you. The Thai people frown at you. You know you are doing something wrong. What is it?

    a. Only Thai people sit on the ground at temples. People from other countries should stand or sit on a chair.

    b. Your back is against the wall of the temple. It is against the law to touch any part of a temple in Thailand.

    c. You are sitting with your feet stretched out in front of you. That means you are pointing your feet at people. It is very impolite.

You are in Korea. You get on a crowded city bus. There is no place to sit, so you stand. You are holding a big package. A woman who is sitting near you pulls at your package. What should you do?

    a. The woman is trying to tell you that it is illegal to get on a crowded bus with a big package. Get off the bus at the next stop and take a taxi.

    b. The woman wants to help you. Give her your package and smile.

    c. Thieves are common on crowded city buses. Hold on to your package tightly.

You are shopping in France. You are carrying a shopping bag full of things you bought at a department store. You walk into a small shop and look around. You don't see anything you want, so you leave. As you are leaving, you see that the shop owner is frowning at you. What have you done wrong?

    a. You carried your shopping bag around the small shop. You should have given it to the shop owner to hold for you.

    b. You were impolite. You didn't say "Bonjour" when you entered the shop, and you didn't say "Au revoir" when you left.

    c. You didn't buy anything. You should have bought something small, just to be polite.

You are at a tea shop in Nepal. The man next to you—a Nepali—pays five rupees for his cup of tea and leaves. When you get up to leave, the shop owner tells you the price of your cup of tea is seven rupees. What do you do?

    a. Be firm. Tell the shop owner you saw the other man pay only five rupees. Say that you'll pay only five rupees, too.

    b. Try to bargain the price down to at least six rupees.

    c. Ask again how much the tea is. If the shop owner says seven rupees again, pay the seven rupees.

You are studying at a university in the United States. In line at the cafeteria, you meet a friendly American student. You have a long conversation. You are new in the United States and lonely. Here, you think, is a real friend. You exchange phone numbers, but your new friend doesn't call you. A week later, you see her again in the cafeteria. She smiles and says, "Hi," but she passes by your table to sit with some friends. What should you do?

    a. Walk over to her table. Ask her, "Why didn't you call me?"

    b. Forget her. She probably doesn't want to make new friends.

    c. Call her once or twice. Invite her to do something together. If she always says she is busy, then forget her.

You have just moved to the United States. You want cable and high-speed Internet access installed in your apartment as soon as possible. What should you do?

    a. Call the cable company. Take the first appointment that is available.

    b. Go to the cable company. Explain how important it is for you to get Internet access as soon as possible.

    c. Ask people if they know anyone who works at the cable company. When you have the name of a cable company employee, call the employee. Ask him/her to move your name to the top of the list.

You are living in Malaysia. You have a puppy. You have invited a Malaysian family, who are Muslim, to your house. What should you do about your puppy?

    a. Put the puppy in another room, out of sight.

    b. Invite your Malaysian guests to play with the puppy.

    c. Be sure to tell your Malaysian guests that the puppy doesn't bite.

You are living in Italy. An Italian family invites you to visit them at 5:00 P.M. Two hours later, you and the family are still laughing and talking. They invite you to stay for dinner. You have no plans for dinner. You should say,

    a. "Yes, thank you," and stay.

    b. "Yes, thank you, but only if I can help prepare dinner."

    c. "Thank you, but I can't tonight. Let's get together for dinner another time."

You are living in Spain. You have to sign a paper in the presence of a notary public. So, you make an appointment with a notary public for 10:00 A.M. When you arrive at 10:00, a receptionist politely asks you to take a seat. At 11:30, you are still waiting for the notary. What should you do?

    a. Tell the receptionist that you can't wait any longer. Ask her to take you to the notary public's office immediately.

    b. Walk past the receptionist and knock on the notary public's door.

    c. Keep quiet and keep waiting.

At a party in France, you are introduced to a stranger. What is a good question to begin a conversation?

    a. "Are you married?"

    b. "What kind of work do you do?"

    c. "Have you seen the new Monet exhibit at the Orsay Museum?"

UNIT 4

1. PRE-READING

The fish in the picture have needles in their backs because they are getting acupuncture.

Just for fun, test your knowledge of acupuncture. Read the statements below. If you think the statement is true, circle *T*. If you think the statement is false, circle *F*. If you aren't sure, take a guess.

1. Acupuncture for goldfish is common in Asia.	T	F
2. A doctor who uses acupuncture is an acupractor.	T	F
3. All acupuncture needles are 1 inch (2.5 centimeters) long.	T	F
4. Acupuncture is very painful.	T	F
5. Acupuncture needles must stay in place for two hours.	T	F
6. Acupuncture needles always go in the place where the patient has pain.	T	F
7. The Japanese were the first to use acupuncture.	T	F

Now check your answers in the Answer Key.

Healthy Again

Mr. Cho was worried. Something was wrong with his goldfish. They had red patches on their skin, they weren't eating, and they didn't have much energy. Mr. Cho thought the fish probably had an infection. To cure the infection, he stuck needles into the backs of the fish. That may seem unusual to some people, but it didn't seem unusual to Mr. Cho. Mr. Cho is an acupuncturist—a person who uses needles to treat illness and pain.

Mr. Cho left the needles in the fish for several minutes and then took them out. During the next few days, he repeated the treatments. Soon the fish began to feel better. They swam with more energy and started to eat again, and the red patches on their skin disappeared. Did the fish get better because of the acupuncture treatments? Mr. Cho thinks so.

Although acupuncture for goldfish is uncommon, acupuncture for people is very common in Asia. Acupuncturists there help people who have medical problems such as infections, backaches, and stomachaches. They even use acupuncture during operations so that patients won't feel pain.

To see what happens during an acupuncture treatment, let's imagine that Ming, a man who often has headaches, decides to go to Dr. Han, an acupuncturist. This is what might happen at Dr. Han's office.

First, Dr. Han examines Ming and asks him about his headaches. There are many kinds of headaches, and Dr. Han needs to know what kind of headaches Ming has.

Then Dr. Han decides where to insert the needles. Ming is surprised when Dr. Han tells him that she will insert needles in his neck and foot, but none in his head. That is not unusual. Often acupuncture needles are not inserted in the place where the patient feels pain.

Next, Dr. Han chooses the needles, which range in size from ½-inch long to 6 inches. Dr. Han chooses 1-inch needles for Ming and begins to insert them. Ming feels a little pinch when each needle goes in. That is not unusual either. Some patients say it hurts a little when the needles go in; other patients say it doesn't hurt at all. The needles stay in place for fifteen minutes. Then Dr. Han removes them. Before he goes home, Ming makes an appointment to see Dr. Han in a week. Dr. Han says that Ming will know in a few weeks if the treatments are working.

Acupuncture has helped millions of people—not only in Asia, but all over the world. People say that acupuncture works. But *how* does it work?

One explanation of how acupuncture works is thousands of years old. The ancient Chinese, who were the first to use acupuncture, believed that energy flowed through the human body. They thought that sometimes too much energy—or too little energy—flowed to one part of the body. That caused pain or sickness. There were, however, several hundred places on the body where an acupuncturist could change the flow of energy. Those places were called acupuncture points. A needle inserted into an acupuncture point on a patient's leg, for example, changed the flow of energy to the patient's stomach. When the energy flowed correctly again, the patient would feel better.

There are also several modern explanations of how acupuncture works. Scientists point out that the acupuncture points have many more nerve endings than other places on the skin. Nerve endings receive pain messages when someone is sick or hurt. The pain messages then travel through the nerves. Perhaps acupuncture also sends messages through the nerves. These messages interrupt pain messages that are on their way to the brain. Because the pain messages never reach the brain, the patient feels better. Or perhaps the numb feeling some patients experience after acupuncture is simply the body's normal reaction to injury.

People who have been helped by acupuncture probably don't care which explanation is correct. They are just happy to be like Mr. Cho's fish—healthy again.

2. VOCABULARY

◆ **LOOKING AT THE STORY**

Read each sentence. What is the meaning of the word(s) in italics? Circle the letter of the correct answer.

1. The fish had red *patches* on their skin.
   a. places that looked different from the area around them
   b. places where acupuncturists insert needles

2. Mr. Cho wanted to *cure the infection*.
   a. learn about the fish
   b. make the sickness go away

3. He *stuck* needles into the backs of the fishes.
   a. threw
   b. pushed

4. An acupuncturist is a person who uses needles to *treat* illness and pain.
   a. try to cure
   b. cause

5. During the next few days, he *repeated the treatments*.
   a. watched his fish very carefully
   b. stuck needles into the backs of the fishes again

6. Acupuncture for fish is *uncommon*.
   a. difficult
   b. unusual

7. Dr. Han decides where to *insert* the needles.
   a. put in
   b. buy

8. The needles *range in size* from ½-inch long to 6 inches.
   a. The smallest needles are ½-inch, the largest are 6 inches, and there are other sizes in between.
   b. The needles come in two sizes: ½-inch and 6 inches.

9. The ancient Chinese believed that energy *flowed* through the human body.
   a. escaped
   b. traveled

10. These messages *interrupt* pain messages that are on their way to the brain.
    a. stop
    b. help

◆ **LOOKING AT SPECIAL EXPRESSIONS**

Find the best way to complete each sentence. Write the letter of your answer on the line.

to point out = to draw attention to; to say "Look at this." or "Think about this."

_____ 1. Scientists point out that acupuncture points

_____ 2. He pointed out that the bus we wanted to take

_____ 3. The students pointed out that the answers for Unit 9

a. arrived in Chicago in the middle of the night.

b. were missing from the Answer Key.

c. have many more nerve endings than other places on the skin.

3. COMPREHENSION/READING SKILLS

◆ UNDERSTANDING THE MAIN IDEAS

What information is *not* in the story? Draw a line through the information.

1. What was wrong with Mr. Cho's goldfish?
   a. They had red patches on their skin.
   b. They weren't eating.
   c. ~~They had fevers.~~
   d. They didn't have much energy.

2. To treat his fish, Dr. Cho
   a. stuck needles into their backs.
   b. left the needles in for several minutes.
   c. repeated the treatments during the next few days.
   d. gave them medicine.

3. After the acupuncture treatments, Mr. Cho's fish
   a. swam with more energy.
   b. started to eat again.
   c. were sold for a lot of money.
   d. didn't have red patches on their skin anymore.

4. Acupuncturists in Asia use acupuncture
   a. to help people with backaches.
   b. to treat broken bones.
   c. to help people with stomachaches.
   d. during operations so that patients don't feel pain.

5. What happened before Dr. Han inserted the needles?
   a. She told Ming how much the treatment would cost.
   b. She examined Ming and asked him about his headaches.
   c. She decided where to insert the needles.
   d. She chose 1-inch needles.

6. What happened during Ming's acupuncture treatment?
   a. Dr. Han inserted the needles.
   b. Ming felt a little pinch when each needle went in.
   c. Ming walked around the office.
   d. The needles stayed in place for fifteen minutes.

7. What are some explanations of how acupuncture works?
   a. It corrects the energy flow in the body.
   b. It interrupts pain messages on their way to the brain.
   c. It changes the flow of blood through the body.
   d. It causes tiny injuries that make the body feel numb.

◆ UNDERSTANDING SUPPORTING DETAILS

Find the best way to complete each sentence. Write the letter of your answer on the line.

_____ 1. Something was wrong with Mr. Cho's goldfish. For example,

_____ 2. The fish began to feel better. For example,

_____ 3. Acupuncture for people is very common in Asia. For example,

_____ 4. There are several hundred places on the body where an acupuncturist can change the flow of energy. For example,

a. acupuncturists there use acupuncture during operations so that patients don't feel pain.

b. a needle inserted into an acupuncture point on a patient's leg changes the flow of energy to the patient's stomach.

c. they swam with more energy and started to eat again.

d. they had red patches on their skin and they weren't eating.

4. DISCUSSION

Acupuncture is one type of medical treatment. There are many other types of medical treatments. Look at the following seven types of treatments for headaches. Read about the treatments. If you had headaches often, which treatments would you try? For each type of treatment, circle _Yes_ or _No_.

1. Acupuncture	Insert one needle in the neck and another in the foot.	YES	NO
2. Acupressure (also called Shiatsu)	With your fingertips, push on the back of the head and the sides of the forehead. Massage the hand between the thumb and the first finger.	YES	NO
3. Chiropractic	Give a massage; move the bones in the spine so that the spine is straight.	YES	NO
4. Herbalism	Make tea by boiling a special plant or root. Give the tea to the patient, or give a pill made from the plant or root.	YES	NO

5. Holistic Health Care	Treat not only the headache, but also mental or emotional problems that could be causing the person's headache.	YES	NO
6. Spiritual Healing	Pray and put your hands on the person's forehead.	YES	NO
7. Traditional Western Medicine	Give painkillers.	YES	NO

Now work as a class and discuss these questions.

▶ Report your answers to the class by raising your hand. For example, your teacher will ask, "Would you try acupuncture?" If your answer is "yes," raise your hand.

▶ Which treatments would almost everyone in the class try? Which treatments would almost no one try?

▶ Has anyone in the class tried these types of medical treatments? What was the medical problem? Did the treatment work?

5. WRITING

A. **Imagine that you receive a letter from a friend. Your friend writes you that he has a medical problem and is going to try acupuncture. Your friend is afraid because he has never had an acupuncture treatment and doesn't know what will happen. Write a letter to your friend. Tell your friend what happens during an acupuncture treatment.**

B. **Have you ever needed medical treatment? What was the problem? Which type of treatment did you choose? What happened during the treatments? Did you get better? Write about your experience. Here is what one student wrote.**

> A few years ago, I had a painful shoulder and decided to try acupuncture. Before I tried acupuncture, I was afraid of it. I thought, "That looks painful!" When I saw the long needles, I thought they would run through my body. But I was wrong. The needles were long, but the acupuncturist didn't insert the whole needle. He found the place where my shoulder hurt and inserted 30 needles. He inserted the needles little by little, and I didn't feel any pain. I went to the acupuncturist for about a month. After that, my shoulder was better.

In the past ten years, acupuncture has become more common in the West. People are exchanging information about it on the Internet.

Below are three questions that people asked an acupuncture newsgroup on the Internet. Each question is followed by two replies. One reply is generally positive—that is, the person who wrote it had a good experience with acupuncture or knows someone who did. The other reply is generally negative—that is, the person who wrote it had a bad experience with acupuncture or knows someone who did.

Read each e-mail describing a health problem and the two replies that follow it. Put a P next to the reply that is generally positive; put an N next to the reply that is generally negative. Write your answer on the line.

1 ——————————————————————————————————————

Author: Joe Hyer <joehyer@hotmail.com>	post reply ◀ prev next ▶
Subject: Headaches	

I just want to know if anyone has any suggestions because I am at the end of my rope! I have had the same headache for over a year now. I have been to countless neurologists, doctors, and chiropractors. I even went to a special headache clinic. Nothing has worked. Nothing showed up on the CT scan or MRI. All I want to do is get rid of the pain, even if it's just for a day. What can I do? I would appreciate any suggestions you guys give me.

Thank you.

Joe

a. _____

Author: Sheri Beck <beck@ticon.net>	post reply ◀ prev next ▶
Subject: Re: Headaches	

I have a headache/acupuncture story—only it's not really mine, it happened to my mother-in-law. The acupuncturist told her to come in because she had a really bad headache. So she went in. The acupuncturist put some needles in and left. Then he came back and asked if she was feeling any better and she wasn't. He put more needles in and left. Well, he did this several more times— any better, no, more needles. In the meantime she was getting sicker and sicker (headache and stomachache). Finally, the last time he came back in, she said, "Oh, yes, it's much better" just to get those stupid needles out so she could go home and get her medicine. She said she never went back.

Sheri :-)

b. _____

Author: Teri Koop <koop@aol.com>	post reply ◀ prev next ▶
Subject: Re: Headaches	

I know acupuncture doesn't work for everyone, but it was a miracle for me. It did what five years of medications could not. I've been pain-free for six months now—no headaches. It's great and I'd go back in a minute if I even felt the slightest pain again.

Teri

Author: Tony Horton <tony@hort.freeserve.co.uk>
Subject: Does acupuncture hurt?

(post reply) (◄ prev) (next ►)

Tell me the truth . . . Does acupuncture hurt? Even a little bit? How big are the needles, and what do they feel like?

a. _____

Author: Diana Parkinson <diana@brynford.freeserve.uk>
Subject: Re: Does acupuncture hurt?

(post reply) (◄ prev) (next ►)

What acupuncture feels like: It sometimes feels like your skin is being pressed by the tip of a needle (but not puncturing the skin). It sometimes feels like someone has carefully slid a needle just under the very top layer of skin. (Or is it just me that feels that?) I can usually feel something, and sometimes something that I would go so far as to call pain. But it isn't at all severe, and in a way it's that sort of almost nice, tingly sort of pain. My acupuncturist doesn't go into details of what I'm feeling, but he does seem more pleased if I feel something than if I don't. :o) The needles are a couple of inches long, but only up to about ½ inch goes into the skin. Since starting acupuncture, I've come to learn that there is a route back to the "joy of life" I had before. Hope this helps.

b. _____

Author: David James <david_james@bigfoot.com>
Subject: Re: Does acupuncture hurt?

(post reply) (◄ prev) (next ►)

It doesn't actually hurt, but I found it too stressful. When the needles went into my back, I felt my muscles like "paralyze." I was on my stomach, in this horrid trapped position for twenty-five minutes. It was too hard for me, so I quit after five sessions. Afterwards, I felt very relaxed, but during . . . argh! Now I am interested in Chi Gong (sp?). There are no needles with Chi Gong. You make certain movements to move the energy through your body. *****DJ*****

Author: Dan Comstock <dan@mailbag.com>
Subject: Acupuncture for Bad Knees?

(post reply) (◄ prev) (next ►)

I'm a runner, and my knees are giving me trouble. Does anyone have experience with acupuncture for knee problems?

a. _____

Author: SPotter <potter@aol.com>
Subject: Re: Acupuncture for Bad Knees?

(post reply) (◄ prev) (next ►)

My wife had a botched knee surgery that killed a lot of the nerve tissue in her left leg. She was lying in bed screaming and crying for months. We used painkillers, but they didn't help. So we went to an acupuncturist. The acupuncturist said it would cut the healing time in half, which it seemed to, according to an orthopedic surgeon. It was predicted that she would never walk normally again, and now she runs and goes hiking.

b. _____

Author: afjones <afjones@infinet.com>
Subject: Re: Acupuncture for Bad Knees?

(post reply) (◄ prev) (next ►)

My brother-in-law tried acupuncture for his bad knee (football injury), but he ended up having surgery anyway. Many people will tell you of their wonderful experiences with acupuncture. They'll also tell you they saw Elvis Presley at the mall last weekend.

UNIT 5

1. PRE-READING

Look at the picture. Then read these key words from the story.

church	find	Paris
father	girls	photos

What do you think the story is about? Write your guess on the lines below.
Then share your guess with your classmates.

_____

_____

_____

_____

_____

If You Have Time

Natalie Garibian was in her bedroom packing her suitcases. She was 20 years old, and she was both nervous and excited. The next day she was traveling from her home in Florida to Paris, France, where she would study for a semester. She was almost finished packing when her father walked into the room. He held two small black-and-white photos in his hand.

"When I was your age, I traveled, too," he said in Armenian, his native language. "I came to the United States. On the way, I stopped in Syria and stayed with a cousin for a few weeks. She and her husband had four children—a son and three daughters. They're the family in these photos. I heard from a relative that the daughters might be living in Paris now. I know you'll be busy in Paris. But I hope at some point you'll have time to look for these girls. I'd like to know how they are. And I'd like them to meet you."

Mr. Garibian turned the photos over and showed Natalie the names written on the back. "Of course, that was thirty years ago," he continued. "The girls are probably married and have different names. I'm sure they look very different, too. Maybe they don't even live in Paris. Still, I hope you have time to look for them."

Natalie took the photos from her father and sighed. "If I have time, Papa," Natalie answered in Armenian. "If I have time."

Natalie knew that she would have to study hard in Paris. She wanted to travel a little, too. How would she find time to look for the girls? She didn't know what they looked like, what their names were, or where they lived. Looking for them would be like trying to find a needle in a haystack. What was her father thinking? Natalie put the photos at the bottom of her suitcase. She did not intend to spend her semester in Paris looking for the little girls—grown women now— who had met her father thirty years ago.

When Natalie arrived in Paris, she immediately began making the most of her experience. During the week, she went to classes, and on long weekends she took train trips throughout Europe. The summer passed and the fall passed. The days got shorter, darker, and colder. Natalie was homesick. She missed her family. She missed her mother's cooking, and she missed hearing her parents speak Armenian. She remembered seeing a small stone Armenian church on a street in Paris. She decided to go there for a church service, just to hear Armenian spoken again.

When Natalie arrived at the church, she was surprised to see that it was crowded. She found a chair and sat down. A few minutes later, she saw a woman about 70 years old walking up and down the aisle on the other side of the church, looking for an empty chair. The woman was bent over and seemed to have trouble walking. Several people offered her their seats but she shook her head, no, no, and kept walking in Natalie's direction. A few minutes later, she was standing next to Natalie.

Natalie stood up and, in Armenian, offered the woman her seat. The woman sat down. Natalie looked around; the only seat left was at the end of the row, against the stone wall, so Natalie sat down there. All through the service, the woman kept turning her head and staring at her. When the service ended, the woman asked her in Armenian, "You're not from here, are you?"

Natalie was dismayed. She had lived in the United States her whole life, but she had always spoken Armenian with her parents. She thought her Armenian was pretty good. She wondered if she spoke Armenian with an American accent.

"No, I'm not from here," Natalie answered. "How did you know?"

"I'm not from here, either," the woman answered. "I'm visiting my daughters. But I've noticed that the young Armenians, the ones who grow up here, don't speak Armenian. They all speak French. You speak Armenian—good Armenian—so I knew you weren't from here. Where are you from?"

"I'm from the United States, from Florida," Natalie answered.

"Ah, I have relatives in the United States," the woman said. She began to say their names: "Sarkis, Dikran, Ara . . ."

"Ara?" Natalie asked. Ara was Natalie's father's name. "When did you last see Ara?"

(continued)

"Thirty years ago, in Syria," the woman answered. "He stayed with my family for a while on his way to the United States. Such a nice young man. He was so kind to my children."

Natalie began to cry. "That's my father," she said.

The woman began to cry, too, and raised her hands. "Asdoodzo Kordzeh," she said: God's work. "I've been looking for your father for thirty years. I knew you were something special. I knew it in your face."

Natalie had wanted to hear Armenian because she missed her family. She thought they were all thousands of miles away. Not all of them were far away. One of them was sitting near her, in a small stone church in Paris.

2. VOCABULARY

◆ LOOKING AT THE STORY

Read each sentence. Which word or phrase below has the same meaning as the word(s) in italics? Write the letter of your answer on the line.

_k_ 1. Natalie was *putting clothes into* her suitcase.

____ 2. Her father spoke to her in Armenian, his *first* language.

____ 3. Natalie's father knew she couldn't look for the girls immediately. But she was going to be in Paris for a semester. Maybe she could look for them on a weekend or during a holiday. He hoped that she would look for them *sometime*.

____ 4. The children in the photos were *adult* women now.

____ 5. Natalie thought that finding the girls would be *almost impossible*.

____ 6. Natalie didn't *plan* to look for the girls.

____ 7. Natalie was *sad because she missed her home*.

____ 8. Many people in the church asked the woman if she wanted to sit down, but she didn't stop and sit down. She *continued* walking toward Natalie.

____ 9. Natalie stood up and *asked the woman, "Would you like to sit here?"*

____ 10. The old woman *looked at her for a long time*.

____ 11. Natalie thought her Armenian was pretty good, so she was *disappointed* when the woman said, "You're not from here, are you?"

____ 12. As the woman *lifted* her hands, she said, "Asdoodzo Kordzeh."

---

a. homesick	e. offered the woman her seat	i. native
b. dismayed	f. stared at her	j. at some point
c. grown	g. intend	k. packing
d. raised	h. kept	l. like looking for a needle in a haystack

Answer the questions to show that you understand the meanings of the new words. (You don't need to write complete sentences.) Then in small groups, take turns sharing your answers.

1. What are the languages of people who are born in your native country?_____

   _____

2. Are you living in a new country? If so, name three things you packed in your suitcase (besides clothes) when you were getting ready to come. _____

   _____

3. Do you have grown children? If so, write their names and ages. _____

   _____

4. When guests come to your home, what do you offer them to eat and drink?_____

   _____

5. What do you intend to do tomorrow? _____

6. What do you intend to do at some point? _____

   _____

7. Name someone or something that would be so difficult to find, it would be like looking for a needle in a haystack. _____

3. COMPREHENSION/READING SKILLS

◆ UNDERSTANDING THE MAIN IDEAS

Answer the questions. Write your answers on the lines. Write complete sentences.

1. Why was Natalie nervous and excited?

   _____

2. How old was she?

   _____

3. What did her father have in his hand?

   _____

4. Who was the family in the photos?

   _____

5. What was written on the back of the photos?

   _____

Now write five questions of your own about the story. Then answer your questions. Begin your questions with one of these words:

Who	When	Why
What	Where	How

1. Q: _____

   A: _____

2. Q: _____

   A: _____

3. Q: _____

   A: _____

4. Q: _____

   A: _____

5. Q: _____

   A: _____

◆ MAKING INFERENCES

Answer the questions. Write your answers on the lines. (The answers are not in the story, so you have to guess at the answers. Any logical guess is correct.)

1. Natalie was both excited and nervous about going to Paris. What do you think she was excited about? What do you think she was nervous about?

   _____

   _____

2. Why do you think Natalie sighed when she took the photos from her father?

   _____

3. Natalie made the most of her experience. During the week, she went to classes, and on long weekends she took train trips. What else do you think Natalie did to make the most of her time in France?

   _____

4. When Natalie arrived at the Armenian church, she was surprised to see that it was crowded. Why do you think she was surprised?

   _____

5. All through the service, the woman kept staring at Natalie. Why do you think she stared at her?

_____

6. The story ends with Natalie meeting her father's cousin. What do you think happens next?

_____

_____

_____

4. DISCUSSION

A. Natalie's immediate family (her parents, brothers, and sisters) was in the United States. Her extended family (aunts, uncles, cousins, grandparents) was in Armenia, Syria, and France.

Where is your immediate family? Put a star (*) on those places on the map. Where is your extended family? Put an X on those places on the map. Then show your map to a partner. Tell your partner about your family members and where they live.

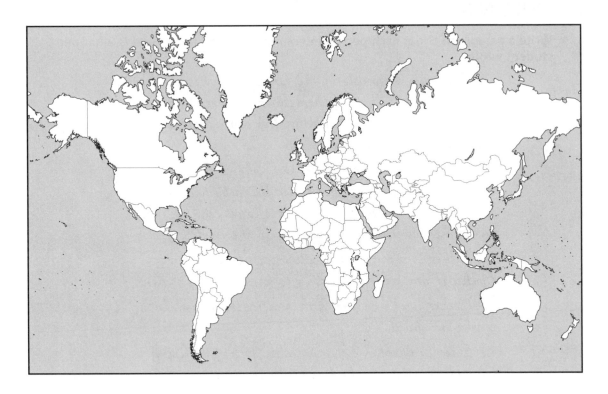

B. Natalie's parents were Armenian, so Natalie spoke Armenian at home.

Interview a partner about the languages your partner's family speaks. Write your partner's answers on the lines. (You do not need to write complete sentences.)

1. What languages does your family speak at home?

_____

2. Do you have children? If so, what language do they speak . . .

with you? _____

with one another? _____

at school? _____

with their friends? _____

3. Which language do you speak . . .

at work? _____

at school? _____

with your friends? _____

5. WRITING

A. Write a paragraph about each person in your immediate family. Here is what one student wrote.

There are six people in my family. The members are Grandmother, Father, Mother, Elder Brother, Younger Brother, and I. We have almost the same faces, but we have different temperaments.

Grandmother is 66 years old. She is strong because she has done almost everything by herself. Her husband died in the war. Now she is retired, but sometimes she helps my parents. So she is still strong.

Father is a farmer. He cultivates flowers with Mother. I am just like him in looks and temperament.

Mother works on the farm and in the house. She works very hard.

Elder Brother is 25 and single. His job is fixing cars. He is quiet, but he has power because he is the oldest. So I follow him.

Younger Brother is 21 and single. He is active and very funny. His job is selling cars. The office of his company is far away from our house, so he lives alone.

B. Natalie's father showed her photos of a family. The photos brought back memories of his time with them.

In the photo frame here, draw a scene from your past that brings back happy memories. (Don't worry if you can't draw well.)

Write a paragraph about the scene. For example, one student drew a picture of herself and her father at the zoo and wrote this paragraph:

When I was a child, my father was very busy. So he rarely played with me. One Father's Day I drew a picture of his face. When I gave it to him, he smiled and said, "Thank you." That was all. But the next Sunday, he took me to the zoo. It was the first time we went out together. He stopped in front of the tigers for a long time, maybe 30 minutes. We were both born in the year of the Tiger. It was a silent and warm time. I remember it clearly.

Two university professors studied children like Natalie, who is the child of immigrants to the United States. Some of the children were born in the United States, and some came when they were small children. The professors begin their book *Legacies: The Story of the Immigrant Second Generation* by describing twelve immigrant children and their families. Following are three of the stories. The names of the children are fictitious, but the stories are true.

Read the stories.

 Alice

Alice lives with her parents, sister, and two brothers in a rented two-bedroom apartment. Her two brothers sleep in the living room and Alice shares a bedroom with her sister. Although the apartment is small, it is tidy and has new furniture.

In their native country, Alice's mother worked for an insurance company and her father ran his own farm. But in the United States, her mother works as a waitress and her father delivers pizzas. They have both applied for green cards—which would make them permanent residents of the United States—but they have not received them yet.

Until they have their papers, they have to work at whatever jobs they can find.

Alice is fluent in English, forgetting her parents' language, and dreams of a brilliant American life. She gets excellent grades and is determined to go to college. Alice was not born in the United States, so she might not be eligible for college scholarships. Her parents don't know how they could possibly pay for a college education. Her mother says, "When children don't want to continue studying, that's one thing; you don't worry too much. But when you have a child who clearly has ambition, and you can't support her, it breaks your heart."

 Jack

Jack came to the United States with his parents when he was 8 years old. By the time he was 13, he felt totally American. He thought his parents were old-fashioned and authoritarian. They complained about his poor grades in school, talked about their own hard life, and told him he had to do better.

One day as Jack and his father were leaving the supermarket, his father asked him to carry the groceries to their old car and wait for him there while he ran another errand. "I'm not your slave," Jack replied. "Carry them yourself."

Jack's father responded as his own father would have in his native country: He slapped Jack twice on the side of his head and shook him by the shoulders. "Until you grow up, you'll do as you're told," he told his son.

Jack carried the groceries, but when he arrived at home, he called the police. His father was taken to the police station and charged with child abuse. Later, the father appeared before a judge who spoke the father's language. He did not send the father to jail but warned him that customs were different in the United States.

Jack's parents sent him back to their native country, where he is living with his grandparents and attending a private school. He cried and protested at first, but he is doing fine now.

His father says, "The U.S.A. is the strangest country in the world: the richest and most powerful, but twisted in knots as far as children are concerned. We had to send him back. We were losing him."

Kate is a 19-year-old university student. She came to the United States when she was 7 years old. She and her eight brothers and sisters all do well in school. She says they were inspired by their older brother and tells this story:

"We were really not interested in school until my oldest brother graduated third in his high school class. That sort of opened our eyes. There was not much pressure to do very well until then, but once my brother did so well, that started us off . . . and everybody followed. The key thing is how the older ones start off, because if the older children start off on the wrong foot, it's very hard to get the younger ones on the right track. I have seen that happen, even to my relatives."

In Kate's family, the older brothers and sisters are responsible for helping the younger ones, so the entire family is a mini school system. Her second-oldest brother graduated from high school as class valedictorian, her third-oldest brother graduated fourth in his class, and Kate was class valedictorian. She says there is both cooperation and competition in her family. "We all urge one another to do better. It creates a good atmosphere. And helping my younger brothers and sisters gives me a good feeling."

Kate is a freshman at the University of California majoring in chemistry. She says she hasn't done as well at the university as she had hoped, partly because there are a lot of students from her native country. She says they are very competitive, and they're almost all studying engineering, science, or math because they can't compete against Americans in English-based courses.

She says, "In my native country, you were taught at a much faster pace. I remember the things that I learned there in second grade were not taught in the United States until fourth or fifth grade. Math is the language we know, where we don't feel handicapped."

Kate wants to be a doctor.

On your own paper, make a chart like this:

Sentences from the Stories	My Responses

Choose three sentences from the stories that you would like to respond to. Copy the sentences word for word in the left column. In the right column, write a response to each sentence. For example, you can write that the sentence

▶ surprised you   ▶ made you feel happy, sad, or angry

▶ confused you   ▶ reminded you of your own experience

Or you can write that you agree or disagree with the opinion expressed in the sentence. Be sure to explain your responses.

UNIT
6

1. PRE-READING

Look at the picture and think about these questions. Discuss your answers with your classmates.

▸ What do you see in the picture? What do you think happened?

▸ The picture was taken at Pompeii. Where is Pompeii? Do you know what happened there? Tell your classmates what you know.

The Buried City

Every year thousands of tourists visit Pompeii, Italy. They see the sights that Pompeii is famous for—its stadiums and theaters, its shops and restaurants. The tourists do not, however, see Pompeii's people. They do not see them because Pompeii has no people. No one has lived in Pompeii for almost 2,000 years.

Once Pompeii was a busy city of 22,000 people. It lay at the foot of Mount Vesuvius, a grass-covered volcano. Mount Vesuvius had not erupted for centuries, so the people of Pompeii felt safe. But they were not safe.

In August of the year 79, Mount Vesuvius erupted. The entire top of the mountain exploded, and a huge black cloud rose into the air. Soon stones and hot ash began to fall on Pompeii. Then came a cloud of poisonous gas. When the eruption ended two days later, Pompeii was buried under 20 feet of stones and ash. Almost all of its people were dead.

Among the dead was a rich man named Diomedes. When the volcano erupted, Diomedes decided not to leave his home. The streets were filled with people who were running and screaming. Diomedes was probably afraid that he and his family would be crushed by the crowd. So Diomedes, his family, and their servants—sixteen people altogether—took some food and went down to the basement. For hours they waited in the dark, hoping the eruption would end. Then they began to cough. Poisonous gas from the mountain was filling the city. Diomedes realized that they had to leave. He took the key to the door, and a servant picked up a lantern. Together they walked upstairs. But the poisonous gas was already filling the house. When they were a few feet from the door, Diomedes and his servant fell to the floor and died. The other fourteen people downstairs died embracing one another.

For centuries, Diomedes and his family lay buried under stones and ash. Then, in the year 1861, an Italian archaeologist named Giuseppe Fiorelli began to uncover Pompeii. Slowly, carefully, Fiorelli and his men dug. The city they found looked almost the same as it had looked in the year 79. There were streets and fountains, houses and shops. There was a stadium with 20,000 seats. Perhaps most important of all, there were many everyday objects. These everyday objects tell us a great deal about the people who lived in Pompeii.

Many glasses and jars had a dark blue stain in the bottom, so we know that the people of Pompeii liked wine. They liked bread, too; metal bread pans were in every bakery. In one bakery oven, there were eighty-one round, flat loaves of bread—a type of bread that is still sold in Italy today. Tiny boxes filled with a dark, shiny powder tell us that the women liked to wear eye makeup, and the jewelry tells us that pearls were popular in the year 79. Graffiti was everywhere in Pompeii. On one wall, someone wrote "Romula loves Staphyclus." On another wall, someone wrote "Everyone writes on these walls—except me."

Fiorelli's discoveries tell us a lot about the way the people lived. They also tell us a lot about the way they died.

One day, Fiorelli was helping his men dig. When he tapped on the hard ash, he heard a hollow sound. He suspected that the space beneath was empty. As an experiment, he drilled a few holes in the ash and poured liquid plaster down the holes. When the plaster was hard, Fiorelli cleared away the ash. He found the plaster form of a man. The man's body had turned to dust long ago, but the ash had hardened around the space where the body had been.

During the following years, Fiorelli filled dozens of spaces with plaster. The plaster forms show how the people of Pompeii looked in their last moments of life. Some have calm expressions on their faces; others look very afraid. Some people died holding their children. Others died holding gold coins or jewelry. Diomedes died with a silver key in his right hand, and his servant died holding a lantern.

Giuseppe Fiorelli, too, has died, but his work continues. One-fourth of Pompeii has not been uncovered yet. Archaeologists are still digging, still making discoveries that draw the tourists to Pompeii.

2. VOCABULARY

◆ LOOKING AT THE STORY

Read each sentence. What is the meaning of the word(s) in italics? Circle the letter of the correct answer.

1. Pompeii was *buried under* 20 feet of stones and ash.
   a. covered by
   b. hit by

2. Diomedes, his family, and their *servants* went down to the basement.
   a. the people who worked in their home
   b. the people who visited Pompeii

3. A servant picked up a *lantern*.
   a. light
   b. knife

4. The other fourteen people downstairs died *embracing one another*.
   a. holding one another
   b. arguing with one another

5. Slowly, carefully, Fiorelli and his men *dug*.

   a.
   b.

6. There were streets and *fountains*, houses and shops.

   a.
   b.

7. There was a *stadium* with 20,000 seats.
   a. large indoor theater
   b. large sports field with rows of seats around it

8. There were also everyday *objects* that tell us a great deal about the people who lived in Pompeii.
   a. ideas
   b. things

9. There were many glasses and jars with a dark blue *stain* in the bottom.
   a. juice made from purple grapes
   b. spot that can't be removed

10. *Graffiti* was everywhere in Pompeii.
    a. writing on the walls
    b. garbage

11. When he *tapped on* the hard ash, he heard a hollow sound.
    a. hit lightly
    b. listened to

12. He *suspected that* the space beneath was empty.
    a. told everyone that
    b. thought that probably

Complete the sentences to show that you understand the meanings of the new words. Then in small groups, take turns reading your sentences aloud. Ask your classmates questions about their sentences.

1. A sight I would really like to see is _____.

2. My native city is famous for its _____.

3. If I had servants, I would ask them to _____.

4. Someone I often embrace is _____.

5. An everyday object I have that tells a great deal about me is _____.

6. If I were given permission to write graffiti on a city wall, I would write this:

   _____.

7. Someone or something that always makes me feel calm is _____.

3. COMPREHENSION/READING SKILLS

◆ **UNDERSTANDING TIME RELATIONSHIPS**

"The Buried City" describes Pompeii at three different times: around the year 79, in the 1860s, and today. Read the sentences from the story. Decide what time each sentence tells about. Put a check (✔) in the correct column.

	79	1860	Today
1. Pompeii was a busy city of 22,000 people.	✓		
2. Tourists see the sights Pompeii is famous for, but they do not see its people.			
3. Mount Vesuvius erupted.			
4. Giuseppe Fiorelli began to uncover the city.			
5. Jewelry made of pearls was popular.			
6. Diomedes, his servants, and his family died.			
7. Fiorelli poured liquid plaster down the holes in the ash.			
8. Someone wrote "Romula loves Staphyclus" on a wall.			
9. Poisonous gas from the mountain filled the city.			
10. One-fourth of Pompeii is not yet uncovered.			

◆ UNDERSTANDING CAUSE AND EFFECT

Find the best way to complete each sentence. Write the letter of your answer on the line.

_____ 1. Tourists do not see Pompeii's people

_____ 2. The people of Pompeii felt safe

_____ 3. Diomedes decided not to leave his house

_____ 4. We know that the people of Pompeii liked bread

_____ 5. Fiorelli suspected that spaces beneath the ash were empty

a. because he was afraid that he and his family would be crushed by the crowd.

b. because he heard a hollow sound when he tapped on the ash.

c. because Pompeii has no people.

d. because Mount Vesuvius had not erupted for centuries.

e. because Fiorelli found metal bread pans in every bakery.

4. DISCUSSION

A. Draw a map of your native country. Then choose one of the following activities. In a small group, show your map to your classmates and discuss the answers to the questions.

1. Are there any volcanoes in your country? Where are they? Mark them with a small mountain (▲) on your map. Do they erupt sometimes? Have you ever seen a volcanic eruption? Tell your classmates what you saw.

2. The people of Pompeii lived at the foot of a volcano. That was a dangerous place to live. Do people live in dangerous places in your country? Mark the places with an exclamation point (!) on your map. Why are those places dangerous? Why do people live there?

3. Are there places in your country that archaeologists have uncovered or are still uncovering? Mark the places with a star (*) on your map. Tell your classmates about them.

B. When the volcano erupted at Pompeii, people who left took their most important possessions. Imagine that your home is on fire. Everyone who lives with you is safe, but your home will burn to the ground. There is time for you to save three of your possessions. Which possessions will you save?

I will save . . .

1. _____

2. _____

3. _____

Why are the possessions on your list important? Are they expensive? Were they gifts from special people? Are they things you can't buy? Show your list to a partner. Explain why the things on your list are important to you.

5. WRITING

A. Write a description of one possession that is on the list you made in Exercise 4B. Explain why it is important to you. Here is what one student wrote.

If I could save one possession, I would save the letters from my friends.

Before I came to the United States, one of my friends wrote me this letter:

"You will go to the United States soon. You may have many hard times before you adapt to your new environment. But don't forget that I am thinking of you all the time. Even if I'm not close to you, You'll always be in my heart."

Every time I feel homesick, I read his letter. It always cheers me up. How could I ever replace a possession like that?

B. Every year, thousands of tourists visit Pompeii. Have you ever been a tourist? Have you ever visited a beautiful or interesting place in your native country or in another country? Write about it. Here is what one student wrote.

My Visit to Kyoto, Japan

I went to Kyoto in April this year. I stayed in a Japanese-style hotel. A mountain river ran past the hotel, and there was a wooden bridge over the river. From my hotel room, I could see a mountain. The mountain was many colors of green, and at the foot of the mountain, there were many cherry blossoms. The green colors and the cherry blossoms were reflected on the river. It was a beautiful view. My heart softened.

Following are five paragraphs that give more information about the people and places of Pompeii. On page 55, there are five photos.

Read the paragraphs. Then match each paragraph with the photo that fits it best. Write the number of the paragraph below the photo. Be sure to read each paragraph to the end before you make your choice.

1 It appears that when Vesuvius erupted, less-wealthy people tried to leave the city, while wealthy Pompeiians stayed in their houses. The wealthy people were probably afraid that if they left, their houses would be looted when the eruption ended. So, they gathered up their most valuable possessions and ran to the strongest room in the house. When Fiorelli uncovered Pompeii, he sometimes found a whole family and their servants—all skeletons—together in one room of their house. The skeletons were surrounded by jewelry, coins, gold, and silver. In one house, a collection of beautiful silver was found hidden in the basement. All 115 pieces of silver were in perfect condition.

2 Houses in Pompeii did not have bathtubs because bathing was a recreational activity. Pompeii had four public baths, some for men and some for women. The layout of the baths indicates that bathers probably followed this routine: After checking their clothes, visitors took a cool bath to get clean. After the cool bath, they were massaged with fragrant oils. Then they were ready for the next four baths: a bath in warm water, a bath in very hot water (like the water in our Jacuzzis), another bath in warm water, and finally a bath in cool water. After their baths, the visitors could spend some time at the bath's library, swimming pool, or restaurant. Evidently, people stayed at the baths until well into the evening; 1,300 lamps were found at one bath.

3 Imagine driving your car to a city—let's say, Paris—and discovering that you could not drive your car into Paris; you had to leave it parked outside the city. If you wanted to see Paris by car, you had to rent a Parisian car or travel by taxi. That was essentially the situation in Pompeii. Pompeii had a monopoly on transportation within its walls because of the way its streets were constructed. The stone streets of Pompeii filled with water during rainy weather. So that people could cross the streets without getting their feet wet, there were high blocks of stone at each intersection.

The blocks of stone were always placed the same distance apart. Pompeiians knew what that distance was and built their chariots and carts so that the wheels passed on either side of the stepping stones. Few visitors to Pompeii had chariots that fit between the stepping stones, so most travelers had to leave their vehicles at the city gates. Cab drivers did a good business in Pompeii.

4 Visitors to Pompeii are amazed to see that some houses are identified by the owners' names. Signs in front of the houses say, for example, "This was the house of Diomedes" or "This was the house of Quintus Poppaeus." How did archaeologists learn the names of some Pompeiians and figure out exactly where they lived? Actually, it was quite simple. Many Pompeiians were businessmen who kept their business records on wax tablets. Their names were on the tablets. So, if wax tablets labeled "Diomedes" were found in a house, it is almost certain that Diomedes and his family lived there. In some cases, we know not only the names of the people who lived in a house but also what those people looked like. In the house of a man named Jucundus, there was a bronze bust of a man—probably Jucundus himself. We know that Jucundus had big ears, thin hair, wrinkles on his forehead, and a large wart on his left cheek.

5 Pompeiians entertained themselves by watching gladiators fight. Pairs of gladiators, who were slaves or convicted criminals, generally fought until one man died. Gladiators who survived fight after brutal fight became heroes, much like our rock stars and great athletes. (When Pompeii was uncovered, the form of a woman wearing a lot of jewelry was found in the gladiators' barracks. Archaeologists speculate that she had gone there to catch a glimpse of her favorite hero.) The contests of the gladiators were so popular that Pompeiians built a stadium just for the fights. With 20,000 seats, the stadium held almost the entire population of Pompeii.

a. _____

b. _____

c. _____

d. _____

e. _____

UNIT 7

1. PRE-READING

Below are pairs of English words that sound alike. Your teacher will say one word from each pair. Circle the word that you hear.

1. feel	fill		8. thought	taught
2. they	day		9. thick	sick
3. men	man		10. Jell-O	yellow
4. ice	eyes		11. fifteen	fifty
5. cap	cup		12. bomb	bum
6. glass	grass		13. Oakland	Auckland
7. hot	hat			

After you finish this exercise, your teacher will tell you the correct answers. Was the exercise difficult for you? If it was, don't worry—it's difficult for native speakers of English, too. In this story, you will learn how the last two pairs of words caused *big* problems for people whose native language is English.

Misunderstandings

He had uncombed hair, dirty clothes, and only thirty-five cents in his pocket. In Baltimore, Maryland, he got on a bus and headed straight for the restroom. He thought that if he hid in the restroom, he could ride to New York without paying. But a passenger at the back of the bus saw him. She tapped the person in front of her on the shoulder and said, "There's a bum in the restroom. Tell the bus driver." That passenger tapped the person sitting in front of him. "Tell the bus driver there's a bum in the restroom," he said.

The message was passed from person to person until it reached the front of the bus. But somewhere along the way, the message changed. By the time it reached the bus driver, it was not "There's a *bum* in the restroom" but "There's a *bomb* in the restroom." The driver immediately pulled over to the side of the highway and radioed the police. When the police arrived, they told the passengers to get off the bus and stay far away. Then they closed the highway. That soon caused a 15-mile-long traffic jam. With the help of a dog, the police searched the bus for two hours. Of course, they found no bomb.

Two similar-sounding English words also caused trouble for a man who wanted to fly from Los Angeles to Oakland, California. His problems began at the airport in Los Angeles. He thought he heard his flight announced, so he walked to the gate, showed his ticket, and got on the plane. Twenty minutes after takeoff, the man began to worry. Oakland was north of Los Angeles, but the plane seemed to be heading west, and when he looked out his window, all he could see was ocean. "Is this plane going to Oakland?" he asked the flight attendant. The flight attendant gasped. "No," she said. "We're going to *Auckland*— Auckland, New Zealand."

Because so many English words sound similar, misunderstandings among English-speaking people are not uncommon. Not all misunderstandings result in highways being closed or passengers flying to the wrong continent. Most misunderstandings are much less serious. Every day people speaking English ask one another questions like these: "Did you say seven*ty* or seven*teen*?" "Did you say that you *can* come or that you *can't*?" Similar-sounding words can be especially confusing for people who speak English as a second language.

When a Korean woman who lives in the United States arrived at work one morning, her boss asked her, "Did you get a plate?" "No . . . ," she answered, wondering what in the world he meant. She worked in an office. Why did the boss ask her about a plate? All day she wondered about her boss's strange question, but she was too embarrassed to ask him about it. At five o'clock, when she was getting ready to go home, her boss said, "Please be on time tomorrow. You were fifteen minutes late this morning." "Sorry," she said. "My car wouldn't start, and . . . " Suddenly she stopped talking and began to smile. Now she understood. Her boss hadn't asked her, "Did you get a plate?" He had asked her, "Did you get up late?"

English is not the only language with similar-sounding words. Other languages, too, have words that can cause misunderstandings, especially for foreigners.

An English-speaking woman who was traveling in Mexico saw a sign in front of a restaurant. The sign said that the special that day was "*sopa con jamón y cebollas*." She knew that was Spanish for "soup with ham and onions." That sounded good. As the woman walked to her table, she practiced ordering. She whispered to herself, "*Sopa con jamón y cebollas. Sopa con jamón y cebollas.*" Then she sat down, and a waiter came to take her order. "*Sopa con jabón y caballos*," she said. "What?" the waiter asked. No wonder the waiter didn't understand. The woman had just ordered a very unusual lunch: soup with soap and horses.

Auckland and *Oakland*. "A plate" and "up late." *Jamón* and *jabón*. When similar-sounding words cause a misunderstanding, probably the

(continued)

best thing to do is just laugh and learn from the mistake. Of course, sometimes it's hard to laugh. The man who traveled to Auckland instead of Oakland didn't feel like laughing. But even that misunderstanding turned out all right in the end. The airline paid for the man's hotel room and meals in New Zealand and for his flight back to California. "Oh, well," the man later said, "I always wanted to see New Zealand."

2. VOCABULARY

◆ LOOKING AT THE STORY

Read each sentence. What is the meaning of the word(s) in italics? Circle the letter of the correct answer.

1. She *tapped the person* in front of her *on the shoulder*.
   a. touched the person's shoulder lightly with her hand
   b. pushed hard on the person's shoulder

2. "There's a *bum* in the restroom."
   a. person who doesn't work and probably doesn't have a home
   b. person who travels by bus

3. The driver *pulled over* to the side of the highway.
   a. looked
   b. moved

4. The driver *radioed the police*.
   a. called the police on his radio
   b. got the attention of a police car

5. That soon caused a *15-mile-long traffic jam*.
   a. line of stopped cars that was 15 miles long
   b. line of cars going only 15 miles per hour

6. The police *searched the bus* for two hours.
   a. looked everywhere on the bus
   b. drove everywhere with the bus

7. Twenty minutes after *takeoff*, the man began to worry.
   a. the plane went up into the air
   b. the man took off his jacket

8. "Is this plane going to Oakland?" he asked the *flight attendant*.
   a. person who flies an airplane
   b. person who takes care of the passengers on an airplane

9. Misunderstandings among English-speaking people *are not uncommon*.
   a. never happen
   b. happen often

10. Not all misunderstandings *result in highways being closed*.
    a. mean that highways are closed
    b. cause highways to be closed

11. She *whispered* to herself, "Sopa con jamón y cebollas."
    a. talked very quietly
    b. thought very seriously

12. But even that misunderstanding *turned out all right in the end*.
    a. was OK after the plane turned around
    b. had a happy ending

◆ LOOKING AT SPECIAL EXPRESSIONS

Find the best way to complete each sentence. Write the letter of your answer on the line.

to head straight for = **to go immediately to**

_b_ 1. He got on the bus and

_____ 2. When the children arrived
at the park,

_____ 3. We were hungry, so
when we got home,

a. they headed straight for
the playground.

b. headed straight for the
restroom.

c. we headed straight for the
kitchen.

by the time = **when**

_____ 4. By the time it reached the bus driver,

_____ 5. By the time I got home from the store,

_____ 6. By the time we got to the theater,

d. the message was "There's a
bomb in the restroom."

e. the best seats were taken.

f. the ice cream had melted.

in the world: **The expression is used with a question word to show surprise.**

_____ 7. "No, I didn't get a plate," she answered,
wondering

_____ 8. When the phone rang at 1:00 A.M.,
he wondered

_____ 9. When we told her we were going for
a walk, she asked us

g. why in the world we were
going outside in such bad
weather.

h. who in the world would call at
that hour.

i. what in the world he meant.

no wonder = **it's not surprising**

_____10. No wonder the waiter didn't
understand;

_____11. No wonder you're tired;

_____12. No wonder you didn't do well
on the test;

j. you didn't go to bed until after
midnight last night.

k. the woman had just ordered
a very unusual lunch.

l. you didn't study.

to feel like = **to want to**

_____13. The man who traveled to Auckland
instead of Oakland

_____14. Let's go to the party;

_____15. I'll just eat a sandwich;

m. I feel like dancing.

n. I don't feel like eating a big
dinner.

o. didn't feel like laughing.

3. COMPREHENSION/READING SKILLS

◆ **UNDERSTANDING CAUSE AND EFFECT**

Find the best way to complete each sentence. Write the letter of your answer on the line.

_____ 1. The man hid in the restroom

_____ 2. There was a 15-mile-long traffic jam

_____ 3. The man who wanted to fly to Oakland was worried

_____ 4. The Korean woman didn't ask her boss about his strange question

_____ 5. Her boss asked her, "Did you get up late?"

a. because the police closed the highway.

b. because he didn't want to pay for his bus ride.

c. because she had arrived at work fifteen minutes late.

d. because the plane seemed to be heading west, not north.

e. because she was too embarrassed.

◆ **UNDERSTANDING DETAILS**

Read the sentences from the story. One word in each sentence is _not_ correct. Find the word and cross it out. Write the correct word.

1. He had uncombed hair, dirty clothes, and only thirty-five ~~dollars~~ *cents* in his pocket.

2. In Baltimore, Maryland, he got on a train and headed straight for the restroom.

3. He thought that if he hid in the restroom, he could ride to Washington without paying.

4. But a driver at the back of the bus saw him.

5. She tapped the person in front of her on the foot and said, "There's a bum in the restroom."

Now copy three other sentences from the story, but change one word in each sentence so that the information is _not_ correct. Give your sentences to a partner. Your partner will find the incorrect word in each sentence, cross it out, and write the correct word. When your partner is finished, check the corrections.

6. _____

_____

7. _____

_____

8. _____

_____

4. DISCUSSION

A. Have you ever confused two similar-sounding English words? Which two words did you confuse? What happened?

In a small group, tell your classmates about your experience. The group will choose one story to act out in front of the class (with the permission of the person who told the story). People in the group will volunteer to play roles. The person who told the story will not take a role. He or she will be the "director."

B. In your native language, are there similar-sounding words (like *seventy* and *seventeen*) that people sometimes confuse? What are the words? Tell the class.

C. The message "There's a bum in the restroom" changed as people passed it to the front of the bus. Will a message that is passed around your classroom change, too? To find out, play the telephone game.

One of your classmates (Classmate #1) will whisper a message to a classmate sitting nearby (Classmate #2). The message can be anything, for example, "The weather is nice today, but tomorrow it's going to rain." Classmate #2 will whisper the message to Classmate #3. Classmate #3 will whisper the message to Classmate #4, and so on. (When a classmate whispers the message to you, you may not ask him or her to repeat it. You must pass the message you hear, even if it makes no sense.) The last classmate to hear the message will say it out loud. Is it the same message that Classmate #1 whispered?

5. WRITING

A. "I always wanted to see New Zealand," the man who flew to Auckland said. Is there a place that you've always wanted to see? Why do you want to go there? What sights do you want to see? Write about a place you've always wanted to visit.

B. The woman in the story ordered soup with soap and horses. Have you ever had a misunderstanding about food? Have you ever had a problem eating at someone's house or buying food at a supermarket or ordering food at a restaurant? Write about your experience. Here is what one student wrote.

> On a visit to the United States, I went to a restaurant with my friends. I ordered a salad. The waitress asked me, "What kind of dressing do you want on your salad—blue cheese, ranch, Italian, or French?" Of course, I said "French" because I am French. When the waitress brought the salad, I was shocked. The dressing was orange. I had never seen dressing like that in France. Then I tasted it. It tasted terrible. I never ordered "French" dressing again.

Some English words and phrases sound so similar, they confuse even native speakers—people who have been speaking English all their lives.

Following are some mistakes that people in the United States—all native speakers—made. Which words did they confuse? Look at the words in the box. Write your answers on the lines.

fried egg	sauce	which it stands
ice cream	self-esteem	x-rayed
onion	tennis shoes	youth in Asia
only		

1 A little boy asked his mother to make him a "Friday sandwich." The boy didn't really want a "Friday" between two slices of bread. He wanted a _____ sandwich.

2 A teacher asked a 7-year-old girl if she had any brothers or sisters. "No," the girl answered. "I'm a lonely child." Actually, the expression isn't "a lonely child"; it's "an _____ child."

3 A young woman went to a movie with her boyfriend. As they were driving home, her boyfriend turned to her and said, "I'm going to take you to a place where they have the best diamond rings in the world." The woman was excited. Her boyfriend was going to buy her a diamond ring! A few minutes later, her boyfriend pulled into the drive-thru of a fast-food restaurant. When he ordered the food, the woman realized that her boyfriend hadn't said "the best diamond rings." He had said "the best _____ rings."

4 A little girl named Heather went to a Mexican restaurant with her family. When the waitress put Heather's dinner down in front of her, Heather covered her meal with her hands and told her parents, "Please don't put any hot socks on my food." Actually, it wasn't hot "socks" that Heather didn't like; it was hot _____.

5 A woman who hurt her arm went to the emergency room of a hospital. Doctors checked her arm and told her it was not badly hurt. After the woman left the hospital, a nurse wrote this on the woman's medical chart: "Patient was examined, X-rated, and sent home." Movies are sometimes X-rated, but patients are _____.

6 A teenage girl wrote a letter to her best friend. She told her friend that her boyfriend had broken up with her, and now she didn't feel good about herself. She wrote that he hurt her "self of steam." Actually, the expression "self of steam" doesn't exist in English. She meant to say that the boy had hurt her _____.

7 A teacher asked her students to name famous Americans in history. One boy replied, "Richard Stans." The teacher was puzzled. She had never heard of Richard Stans. "Who is he?" she asked the boy. "I'm not sure," the boy answered, "but he must be very important. Every morning we all stand and face the flag. Then we say, 'I pledge allegiance to the flag of the United States of America, and to the republic for Richard Stans.'" The teacher had to laugh. The boy had misunderstood the correct words, which are: "I pledge allegiance to the flag of the United States of America, and to the republic for _____."

8 A large department store had an optical department where people could get eye exams and buy glasses. One day the optical department was giving free eye exams. So, this was announced over the store's public address system: "The optical department is giving a free eye screening today." A lot of people who were shopping at the store heard the announcement and hurried to the optical department, where a long line formed. It turned out, however, that the people weren't waiting for a free eye screening; they were waiting for free _____.

9 High school students who took a public-speaking class had to give a speech. One student chose as her topic "euthanasia"—the painless killing of people who are incurably sick. After she gave her speech, one student said to another, "Her speech was interesting. But she didn't say anything about teenagers in countries like Japan and China." The student thought the topic of the speech was not "euthanasia" but "_____."

10 A magazine advertised over the radio. The magazine offered a special price of $19.95 for a subscription. For $19.95, people would receive ten issues of the magazine. When some people called the magazine's toll-free number to place their orders, they gave their credit card numbers and then their shoe sizes. Why did they give their shoe sizes? The people had misunderstood the words "ten issues." They thought they were ordering _____.

The words that people confused are listed side by side in the Answer Key. Ask a native speaker of English to read the words aloud. Can you hear any difference in the pronunciation?

1. PRE-READING

Look at the picture and think about these questions. Discuss your answers with your classmates.

▶ What is a thrift store?

▶ Have you ever been to a thrift store? What things were for sale there? Tell your teacher. Your teacher will make a list on the board.

▶ In your native country, do you have thrift stores or other places where you can buy things cheaply? Describe them to your classmates.

▶ The men in the picture are looking at something that one of the men bought at a thrift store. What do you think it is? Why do you think the man on the right looks happy?

A Real Bargain

In his spare time, Ed Jones likes to shop at thrift stores. He looks for things that might be valuable—old dishes or used books, for example. If he finds something valuable, he buys it cheaply and then resells it to an antique dealer.

One day Mr. Jones was shopping at a thrift store in Indianapolis, Indiana, and not having much luck. He didn't see anything he wanted, so he started walking toward the door. Then something caught his eye. Leaning against a wall there was a large cardboard map. He walked over for a closer look.

The map was covered with dust, so Mr. Jones wiped it with his handkerchief. Under the dust was a color map of Paris. It looked old. On the back of the map, someone had written the price: $3. Mr. Jones was quite certain that the map was worth more than $3, so he bought it. He thought he could probably sell it for $40.

Later, at home, Mr. Jones looked more closely at the map. He decided it might be very old. Maybe it was worth even more than $40.

The next day, Mr. Jones took the map to a geography professor at a nearby university. The professor was a map expert. After looking at the map for a few minutes, he became very excited. "I've read about this map!" he exclaimed. Then he told Mr. Jones what he knew.

In 1671, the king of France, Louis XIV, asked a cartographer to make a map of Paris. The cartographer worked on the map for four years. The map he drew was beautiful—it was not just a map, but a work of art as well. The cartographer made several black-and-white copies of the map. Then he carefully colored one of the copies, using blue for rivers, green for trees, and brown for buildings. The professor said that one black-and-white copy of the map was in the British Museum in London, and another was in the Bibliothèque Nationale in Paris. "I think," the professor told Mr. Jones, "that you've just found the color copy of the map—in a thrift store in Indianapolis!" The professor suggested that Mr. Jones take the map to New York City. Experts there could tell Mr. Jones if the professor was right.

The New York experts said the professor was right. They told Mr. Jones that he had the only color copy of the map and that it was extremely valuable. "How much do you think it's worth?" Mr. Jones asked the experts. "Millions," they replied. "It's impossible to say exactly how much the map is worth. It's worth whatever someone is willing to pay for it."

Soon Mr. Jones discovered how much people were willing to pay for the map. Someone offered him $10 million; then someone else immediately offered him $12 million. The most recent offer was $19.5 million. Mr. Jones hasn't decided whether he will sell his $3 map at that price or wait for a higher offer. He is thinking it over.

But how in the world did this map find its way to a thrift store in Indianapolis? Here is what some experts think: The map was probably in a museum or in the home of a wealthy family in France. Then, a thief stole it, perhaps during the confusion of World War I or World War II. The thief sold the map to an antique dealer in France. The French antique dealer, not knowing how valuable the map was, sold it to an antique dealer in Indianapolis. That antique dealer, who also did not know its value, gave it to a neighbor. For ten years, the map hung on a wall in the neighbor's house. Then the neighbor got tired of it and sold it to the thrift store. The map sat in the thrift store for months. Finally Mr. Jones discovered it.

When Mr. Jones went shopping at the thrift store, he was looking for a bargain. He wanted to find something that was worth more than the price he paid. He paid $3 for the map, and it is worth at least $19.5 million. Now, that's a bargain!

2. VOCABULARY

◆ LOOKING AT THE STORY

Read each sentence. What is the meaning of the word(s) in italics? Circle the letter of the correct answer.

1. Ed Jones was shopping at a *thrift store*.
   - (a.) store that sells used things at low prices
   - b. store that sells expensive things at high prices

2. If he found something valuable, he could resell it, perhaps to an *antique dealer*.
   - a. person who fixes broken things
   - b. person who buys and sells old things

3. Leaning against a wall of the store there was a large *cardboard* map.
   - a. made of heavy paper
   - b. made of plastic

4. Mr. Jones was quite *certain* that the map was worth more than $3.
   - a. worried
   - b. sure

5. The next day, Mr. Jones took the map to a *geography* professor at a nearby university.
   - a. the study of the world's countries, cities, oceans, rivers, and mountains
   - b. the study of the world's history, languages, and customs

6. The professor was a map *expert*.
   - a. person who draws maps
   - b. person with special knowledge

7. "I've read about this map!" he *exclaimed*.
   - a. said with strong feeling
   - b. said very quietly

8. Louis XIV asked a *cartographer* to make a map of Paris.
   - a. person who draws maps
   - b. person who writes books

9. The New York experts told Mr. Jones that his map was *extremely* valuable.
   - a. not really
   - b. very

10. "How much do you think it's worth?" Mr. Jones asked the experts. "Millions," they *replied*.
    - a. answered
    - b. asked

11. Someone *offered him $10 million*.
    - a. said, "Will you take $10 million for the map?"
    - b. told him, "I think your map is worth $10 million."

12. Some experts think the map was probably in a museum or in the home of a *wealthy* family in France.
    - a. famous
    - b. rich

13. When Mr. Jones went shopping at the thrift store, he was looking for a *bargain*.
    - a. something that can be bought cheaply
    - b. something that has been used

◆ LOOKING AT SPECIAL EXPRESSIONS

Find the best way to complete each sentence. Write the letter of your answer on the line.

to catch someone's eye = **to get someone's attention**

_b_ 1. Mr. Jones was walking toward the door

_____ 2. She was leaving the museum

_____ 3. He was walking through the department store

a. when a painting by Renoir caught her eye.

b. when a large cardboard map caught his eye.

c. when a sweater caught his eye.

to be worth = **to have a value of**

_____ 4. Mr. Jones was quite certain that

_____ 5. They paid $80,000 for their house, but

_____ 6. He tried to sell his old TV for $500, but nobody bought it because

d. the map was worth more than $3.

e. it wasn't worth more than $250.

f. it was worth at least $100,000.

to be willing to = **to be ready to**

_____ 7. The map was worth whatever

_____ 8. Our teacher said that

_____ 9. I won't have to take the bus home because

g. he was willing to give us extra help after class.

h. my friend is willing to give me a ride.

i. someone was willing to pay for it.

to get tired of = **to become no longer interested in**

_____ 10. The neighbor got tired of the map and

_____ 11. He got tired of hamburgers

_____ 12. I'm getting tired of studying French;

j. after eating them every day for a month.

k. sold it to a thrift store.

l. maybe I'll study Spanish next year.

3. COMPREHENSION/READING SKILLS

◆ UNDERSTANDING CAUSE AND EFFECT

Find the best way to complete each sentence. Write the letter of your answer on the line.

_____ 1. Ed Jones went to the thrift store

_____ 2. He wiped the map with his handkerchief

_____ 3. The professor suggested that Mr. Jones take the map to New York City

_____ 4. Experts in New York said the map was extremely valuable

_____ 5. The map was a bargain

a. because experts there could tell Mr. Jones if the professor was right.

b. because it was cheap but very valuable.

c. because he was looking for a bargain.

d. because it was the only color copy.

e. because it was covered with dust.

Read the sentences from the story. One word in each sentence is *not* correct. Find the word and cross it out. Write the correct word.

1. The map was covered with ~~paint~~ *dust*.

2. When Mr. Jones wiped the map clean, he found a color map of Rome.

3. The map looked new.

4. On the back of the map, someone had written the price: $30.

5. The next day, Mr. Jones took the map to a mathematics professor at the university.

Now copy three other sentences from the story, but change one word in each sentence so that the information is *not* correct. Give your sentences to a classmate. Your classmate will find the incorrect word in each sentence, cross it out, and write the correct word. When your classmate is finished, check the corrections.

6. _____

_____

7. _____

_____

8. _____

_____

4. DISCUSSION

A. Have you—or has anyone you know—ever had an experience similar to Mr. Jones's experience? Have you ever bought something at a low price and then discovered it was worth more than you paid for it? Have you ever had the opposite experience? Have you ever bought something at a high price and then discovered that it was worth less than you paid for it?

Tell your classmates about your experience.

B. The word *bargain* is both a noun and a verb. *A bargain* is something that is bought at a cheap price, like Mr. Jones's map. *To bargain* is to talk in order to get a good price.

Imagine this: You are at an open-air market. You see something you want to buy and you ask about the price. It is too high, so you start to walk away. The seller starts to bargain with you. What does the seller say? What do you say?

Write a conversation between you and the seller. Each person should speak six to eight times. Practice the conversation with a partner and then read it in front of the class.

5. WRITING

A. **What would you do if, like Mr. Jones, you suddenly had $19.5 million? How would you use the money? Make a list of what you would do.**

1. _____

2. _____

3. _____

4. _____

5. _____

B. Imagine that you went to a thrift store and bought something cheaply. The object could be jewelry, a book, a painting, a photograph, a toy, a vase—or anything else that you want it to be. Imagine that later you discovered that the object you bought is very valuable—that it's worth much, much more than you paid for it.

Write a story. In the story, describe what you bought, tell what it's really worth, and explain why it's valuable. Here is what one student wrote.

I bought a dress at a thrift store. It was red and made of lace. It was only $1.

I wore the dress to a party. A woman at the party stared at me for a long time. Then she asked me, "Where did you get that dress?" "I got it from a friend," I answered. That was not true, but I didn't want to say that I had bought it at a thrift store for only $1. "That was Miss K's dress," the woman said. "She wore it at her last concert." (Miss K was a famous singer.) "I'm a great fan of Miss K's," the woman continued. "I have all her CDs, and I have many photographs of her. But I don't have anything that she wore. Will you please sell me that dress? I don't know what your friend paid for it, but I'm willing to pay $500."

I told her she could have the dress for $500 and went home from the party very happy.

Ed Jones's $3 map is worth at least $19.5 million. Can you guess what the items below are worth? All of these valuable items were sold at Christie's, a famous auction house in New York. The most valuable item sold for $3.5 million. The least valuable item sold for $38,000.

Read the descriptions of the items. Then take a guess: Which item do you think sold for $3.5 million? Which one do you think sold for $38,000?

◆ **Letter Handwritten by Abraham Lincoln** ─────────────────

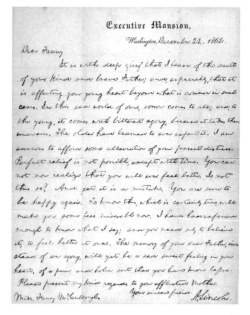

Abraham Lincoln was president of the United States during the Civil War (1861–1865), when the Southern states fought the Northern states over the issue of slavery. The Southern states wanted to separate from the United States.

When the Civil War began, a man named William McCullough wanted to fight for the North. The army rejected him because he was blind in one eye. McCullough had once worked for Lincoln, and he asked the president for help. President Lincoln intervened, and the army accepted McCullough. He was killed in battle.

McCullough's daughter, Fanny, was distraught over her father's death, and Lincoln wrote her a letter of condolence. He began his letter, "It is with deep grief that I learn of the death of your kind and brave father." Then he offered Fanny some comforting words: "You cannot now realize that you will ever feel better. Is this not so? And yet it is a mistake. You are sure to be happy again. To know this, which is certainly true, will make your sorrow less miserable now. I have had experience enough to know what I say; and you need only to believe it, to feel better now."

This is one of Lincoln's most famous letters. It is considered to be one of the greatest condolence letters ever written.

◆ **Andy Warhol Painting** ──────────────────────

The painter Andy Warhol was one of the most influential artists of the twentieth century. He died in New York City in 1987.

Warhol's style of painting is called Pop Art because he took popular, common images and transformed them into art. He painted Coca-Cola bottles, U.S. one-dollar bills, the faces of movie stars, and soup cans. He is perhaps most famous for his soup-can paintings, which he completed in 1961 and 1962. There are thirty-two paintings of soup cans, and each painting is slightly different. This painting is of Campbell's "Pepper Pot" soup.

Margarete Steiff, a German woman, created the first teddy bear more than 100 years ago. Ms. Steiff wasn't originally a toy maker; she was a seamstress who fell into toy-making by chance.

Margarete had polio as an infant, and she was never able to walk. So, when she became a young woman, she needed to find work she could do while sitting in a wheelchair. She decided to become a seamstress. By the time she was 25,

Margarete was earning a good living making dresses for wealthy women.

One day Margarete was looking through a fashion magazine and spotted a pattern for a toy elephant made of cloth. She made several elephants and gave them to friends as gifts. Her friends loved their toy elephants and encouraged Margarete to make more cloth toys. She began making little bears, dogs, and donkeys, and selling them, in addition to selling dresses.

By 1897, Margarete was selling more toys than dresses; in fact, she was selling so many toys, she had to hire forty women to help her sew them. The most popular toys were the cloth bears.

Margarete's nephew took some of the "Steiff bears" to the United States, where they became an instant hit. In the United States, the bears were called "teddy bears," named after President Theodore Roosevelt, whose nickname was Teddy.

The Steiff Company is still in business in Germany. New Steiff teddy bears are quite expensive because they are made by hand. It is the old teddy bears, however—the ones that Margarete Steiff and her forty employees made—that are really valuable. This Steiff teddy bear, which was made in 1905, is in almost perfect condition.

◆ **Diana's Blue Velvet Dress**

In 1997, Diana, Princess of Wales, decided to auction off some of her evening dresses and to give the money to charity. The auction was held at Christie's in New York City in June, two months before her death. On the evening of the auction, the auction house was packed with people, and fifty telephone lines connected the auction to bidders all over the world.

That evening, this blue velvet evening gown brought the highest price. Princess Diana had worn the dress to a dinner at the White House with U.S. President Ronald Reagan and his wife, Nancy. Princess Diana was a fan of Hollywood movies, so the Reagans invited several movie stars to the dinner. After dinner, Diana danced with one of her favorite actors,

John Travolta. The next morning, newspapers all over the world carried photos of Diana dancing in her blue velvet gown.

Check the Answer Key to see how much these items sold for.

1. PRE-READING

Are you superstitious? Read the statements. Then check (✔) *Yes* or *No*.

	YES	NO
1. Black cats are unlucky.		
2. It is unlucky to break a mirror.		
3. If I point at the moon, something bad will happen to me.		
4. It is bad luck when a shoelace breaks.		
5. If my palm itches, I will receive money.		
6. When I want good luck, I sometimes cross my fingers or knock on wood.		
7. I have a lucky number.		
8. I have something that I consider lucky—a lucky pen or a lucky hat, for example.		

If you checked *Yes* after any of these statements, you are probably a little superstitious.

▶ Who in your class is superstitious?

▶ Who in your class is not superstitious?

Black Cats and Broken Mirrors

Do you think that it is bad luck to walk under a ladder or break a mirror? Do you think that black cats and the number 13 are unlucky? The three men in the picture don't. Every Friday the 13th, they walk under ladders, break mirrors, and open umbrellas indoors. They want to prove that they aren't at all superstitious. They may be the only people in the world who aren't. There are more than one million superstitions, and most people believe at least one or two of them.

Many people are superstitious about numbers. They think that there are lucky numbers and unlucky numbers. The number 13 is often considered unlucky. In some parts of the world, buildings have no thirteenth floor and streets have no houses with the number 13. In Japan, the number 4 is considered unlucky because in Japanese, the word *four* is pronounced the same as the word *death*. Japanese never give gifts of four knives, four napkins, or four of anything.

What are lucky numbers? Seven is a lucky number in many places, and the number 8 is considered lucky in Japan and China. In China, businesses often open on August 8 (8/8), and many couples register to get married at eight minutes past eight o'clock on August 8.

Superstitions about numbers are so widespread that some people—called numerologists—make a living giving advice about numbers. In 1937, when the Toyoda family of Japan wanted to form a car company, they asked a numerologist if "Toyoda" would be a good name for the company. The numerologist said it would not be. He explained that "Toyoda" took ten strokes of the pen to write, and 10 was not a lucky number. "Toyota," however, took eight strokes to write, and 8 was a very lucky number. The numerologist recommended "Toyota" as a better name for the company. The family took his advice. As a result, millions of people drive "Toyotas" and not "Toyodas."

In addition to superstitions about numbers, there are many other kinds of superstitions. There are superstitions about eating, sleeping, sneezing, and itching. There are superstitions about animals and holidays and horseshoes. There are even superstitions about superstitions. Those superstitions tell people how to reverse bad luck.

For example, in many parts of the world, spilling salt is bad luck. Throwing salt, however, is good luck. So, people who spill salt throw a little of the spilled salt over their left shoulder. Throwing the spilled salt reverses the bad luck. When the Japanese bump heads, they immediately bump heads again. According to a Japanese superstition, the first bump means their parents will die, but the second bump "erases" the first bump. To reverse bad luck in general, people turn around three times, turn their pockets inside out, or put their hats on backwards. In the United States, baseball players sometimes wear their caps backwards when their team is losing. It looks silly, but the baseball players don't mind if it helps them win the game.

Because there are so many superstitions, it is not surprising that some of them are contradictory. In Germany, it is good luck when the left eye twitches, and bad luck when the right eye twitches. In Malaysia, it is exactly the opposite: A twitching right eye means good luck, and a twitching left eye means bad luck. Accidentally putting on clothes inside out brings good luck in Pakistan but bad luck in Costa Rica. In Chile, unmarried people won't take the last piece of food on the plate because it means they will never marry. In Thailand, unmarried people take the last piece because it means they will marry someone good-looking.

Some superstitions have been with us for so long that they have become customs. In many parts of the world, it is polite to say "Health" or "God bless you" when someone sneezes. People used to think that the soul could escape from the body during a sneeze. They said "God bless you" to protect people from losing their souls. Today, we no longer believe that people who sneeze are in danger of losing their souls, but we say "God bless you" anyway. We say it not because we are superstitious, but because we are polite.

Even people who say they aren't superstitious would probably not do what the men in the picture do—intentionally walk

(continued)

under ladders and break mirrors. Almost everyone is at least a little superstitious. One woman says that when she got married, her aunt gave her white bath towels. "Never buy purple towels," her aunt said. "If you use purple towels, your marriage will end." Does the woman believe that superstition? "No, of course not," she says. "It's silly." Does she use purple towels? "Well, no," she answers. "Why take chances?"

2. VOCABULARY

◆ LOOKING AT THE STORY

Read each sentence. What is (or shows) the meaning of the word(s) in italics? Circle the letter of the correct answer.

1. Do you think that it is bad luck to walk under a *ladder*?
   a. (In the photo on page 72, the man on the right is standing under it.)
   b. (In the photo on page 72, the man in the center is standing under it.)

2. The men walk under ladders and break mirrors to *prove* that they aren't superstitious.
   a. believe it is crazy
   b. show it is true

3. Superstitions about numbers are *widespread*.
   a. found in many places
   b. believed only by children

4. Some people *make a living* giving people advice about numbers.
   a. make money
   b. make mistakes

5. "Toyota" took *eight strokes* of the pen to write.
   a.
   b. メ

6. The family *took his advice*.
   a. did what he suggested
   b. asked for more information

7. There are superstitions that *reverse bad luck*.
   a. change bad luck to good luck
   b. give the bad luck to someone else

8. If you *spill salt*, immediately throw a little of the spilled salt over your left shoulder.
   a. use too much salt
   b. pour out salt accidentally

9. It looks silly, but the baseball players *don't mind* if it helps them win the game.
   a. think that's OK
   b. don't like to think about it

10. Some superstitions *are contradictory*. In Germany, it is good luck when the left eye twitches. In Malaysia, it is bad luck when the left eye twitches.
    a. are very old
    b. mean the opposite

11. Putting clothes on *inside out* brings good luck in Pakistan.
    a. in the house, rather than outside   b. with the inside parts on the outside

12. People used to think that the soul could *escape from* the body during a sneeze.
    a. enter   b. leave

◆ **LOOKING AT SPECIAL EXPRESSIONS**

Find the best way to complete each sentence. Write the letter of your answer on the line.

as a result = **because of that**

___c___ 1. The family took the numerologist's advice. As a result,

_____ 2. He overslept. As a result,

_____ 3. She didn't study. As a result,

a. he was late for work.

b. she didn't do well on the test.

c. millions of people today drive "Toyotas" and not "Toyodas."

in addition to = **as well as** ("In addition to" connects two similar ideas.)

_____ 4. In addition to the superstitions about numbers,

_____ 5. In addition to studying French,

_____ 6. In addition to being an excellent student

d. she's an excellent dancer and swimmer.

e. there are many other kinds of superstitions.

f. he's studying German and Spanish.

according to Mr. Jones = **Mr. Jones says that**

_____ 7. According to a Japanese superstition,

_____ 8. According to my watch,

_____ 9. According to this map,

g. the museum is on Michigan Avenue.

h. the first bumping of heads means your parents will die.

i. it's a quarter to nine.

3. COMPREHENSION/READING SKILLS

◆ **UNDERSTANDING THE MAIN IDEAS**

What information is *not* in the story? Draw a line through the three sentences with information that is not in the story.

▶ The men in the picture want to prove they are not superstitious.

▶ There are over one million superstitions.

▶ Children are usually not superstitious.

▶ Many people are superstitious about numbers.

▶ Numerologists make a living giving people advice about numbers.

▶ It is always a good idea to take a numerologist's advice.

(continued)

▸ Some superstitions tell people how to reverse bad luck.

▸ Some superstitions are contradictory.

▸ Some superstitions have become customs.

▸ People who use purple towels are silly.

▸ Almost everyone is at least a little superstitious.

◆ UNDERSTANDING SUPPORTING DETAILS

Find the best way to complete each sentence. Write the letter of your answer on the line.

_____ 1. Many people are superstitious about numbers. For example,

_____ 2. Some people—called numerologists—make a living giving people advice about numbers. For example,

_____ 3. There are superstitions that tell people how to reverse bad luck. For example,

_____ 4. Some superstitions are contradictory. For example,

_____ 5. Some superstitions have been with us for so long that they have become customs. For example,

a. accidentally putting on clothes inside out brings good luck in Pakistan but bad luck in Costa Rica.

b. it is polite to say "Health" or "God bless you" when someone sneezes.

c. the number 13 is often considered unlucky.

d. throwing spilled salt over the left shoulder reverses bad luck.

e. a numerologist recommended "Toyota" as the name for the car company.

4. DISCUSSION

Form small conversation groups. Ask the people in your group if they know any superstitions about:

salt	garlic	cooking
ladders	four-leaf clovers	eating a pear
mirrors	numbers	dropping silverware
brooms	hiccups	chopsticks
combs	itching	sleeping
knives	sneezing	dreams
shoes	ears ringing	leaving the house
black cats	eye twitching	finding a coin
crows	shivering	opening an umbrella
owls	whistling	knocking on wood
rabbits	cutting nails	weddings
elephants	taking photos	New Year's Day
horseshoes	giving gifts	funeral processions

5. WRITING

A. Make a list of superstitions that some people in your native country believe. Here is an example from a student from Panama.

1. Always sleep with your feet facing the door of your room.
2. If you give your sweetheart a handkerchief or socks, you will argue.
3. If you want a visitor to leave, turn your broom upside down.
4. If a young woman is sweeping the floor and the broom accidentally touches her feet, she will marry a rich old man.
5. To protect yourself from evil spirits, wear your pajamas inside out.

B. Write about something you have that is lucky—a lucky number or a lucky hat, for example. Why is it lucky? Can you remember a time when it brought you good luck? Here is what one student wrote.

When I was a high school student, I had a difficult mathematics test one day. Before the test, our teacher told us, "Use the same pencil you used when you studied last night. When you can't solve a problem, hold the pencil tightly. If you do that, you will be able to solve the problem." I did that, and I got every answer right. I thought, "This is my lucky pencil." But later I discovered that my pencil was lucky only sometimes. When I studied hard, my pencil helped me, but when I didn't study hard, it didn't help me.

C. Has there ever been a time when you've had very good—or very bad—luck? Write about it. Here is what one student wrote.

Last month, I had a very unlucky day. I overslept in the morning because I had forgotten to set my alarm clock. It was raining. On the way to the bus stop, I fell and got wet. Then I missed the bus and was late for my class.

That night a friend of mine called me while I was cooking dinner. It was a long phone call, and I forgot about my dinner. When I finished talking to my friend, I went into the kitchen to check on my dinner. It was burned. I thought, "I have only two hands and one head. I'm trying to do too much." But later I thought, "I was just not lucky today."

Many superstitions and customs that are common in the United States are actually thousands of years old. They have their origins in ancient beliefs.

Read about these ancient beliefs. Then match each ancient belief with one of the modern superstitions or customs listed on the next page. Write the number of your answer on the line.

Long ago, the people who lived in present-day Europe believed that gods lived in trees. Perhaps they came to this conclusion because lightning often strikes trees. Or perhaps they saw trees losing their leaves in the autumn and growing new leaves in the spring and thought that gods and goddesses inside the trees were making these seasonal changes. At any rate, ancient people believed that trees (especially oak trees) had divine power. When people had a favor to ask, they knocked on a tree to let the resident god know they were there and then made their request. If the request was granted, they returned to the tree and knocked a few times to say "thank you."

The ancient Greeks had many gods and goddesses. The goddess of the moon, marriage, and childbirth was Artemis. On Artemis's birthday, people baked moon-shaped cakes and brought them to her temple. They also brought candles to the temple and placed them on the altars there. All the candles were lit and then blown out at the same time. If the people blew out all the candles in one communal breath, Artemis was happy with her worshipers. If some candles remained lit, Artemis was unhappy.

In ancient Asia, people who were sentenced to death were hanged. Sometimes they were hanged from trees, and sometimes they were hanged from the seventh rung of a ladder that was placed against a building. People believed that the space under a ladder that had been used for a hanging was dangerous because the spirit of the dead man could linger there long after the body was gone.

An ancient legend goes something like this: A king with three daughters asks each one to describe how much she loves him. The oldest daughter says she loves him as much as bread. The middle daughter says she loves him as much as wine. The youngest daughter says she loves him as much as salt. The king is furious that his youngest daughter compared her love for him with her love for salt, and he says she must leave the palace. She leaves, but secretly she meets with the palace cook. She asks the cook to leave salt out of her father's meals. The king realizes the importance of salt and calls his youngest daughter back. This story was told by the Romans 2,000 years ago. Salt was important not only to them, but also to people throughout the ancient world. It was used to preserve and flavor food, and it was so valuable that it was considered almost supernatural.

Two thousand years ago, the Etruscans—people who lived in what is now central Italy—used chickens to tell the future. The Etruscans would draw a circle on the ground, divide the circle into sections—one section for each letter of the alphabet—and put kernels of corn in each section. Then they put a chicken in the circle and observed the chicken as it picked up corn. For example, if a young woman wanted to know the first letter of her future husband's name, she would ask that question and then watch to see which section of the circle the chicken went to. After the chicken did its work, it was killed and its collarbone was hung out to dry. Two people then made a wish on the bone. One person held on to one end of the bone while another person held on to the other end. Then both people pulled. When the bone broke, the person left holding the larger piece got his or her wish. (This was called the "lucky break.")

6

Between the Middle Ages and the eighteenth century, witch hunts were common in Europe. People believed they had to find witches and kill them, as witches had the power to do great harm. The suspected "witches" were typically old women who were eccentric and who lived alone. Old women who had cats were especially feared because people believed that cats could be demons who had taken the shape of a cat. The fear of witches eventually subsided, but fear of cats—particularly black cats—remained.

7

Ancient people believed that evil spirits were everywhere, waiting for opportunities to harm people. The spirits were attracted particularly to weddings, where it was easy for them to spot two happy young people—the bride and the groom—and give them bad luck. There was, however, a way to outsmart the evil spirits. Friends of the bride dressed exactly as she was dressed, and friends of the groom dressed exactly as he was dressed. That way, the evil spirits wouldn't know who was getting married.

In the United States today . . .

_____ a. At weddings, the bridesmaids—friends of the bride—usually wear identical dresses, and the groomsmen—friends of the groom—usually wear identical suits.

_____ b. When people talk about their good fortune, they knock on wood to protect their good luck.

_____ c. It is considered unlucky to spill salt, and people who spill it immediately throw a little of the spilled salt over their left shoulder to reverse the bad luck. (They throw the salt over their *left* shoulder because primitive people believed that evil spirits were always on the left.)

_____ d. People believe it is bad luck if a black cat crosses their path.

_____ e. People bake birthday cakes and top them with candles. The person celebrating a birthday tries to blow out all the candles in one breath for good luck.

_____ f. People are afraid to walk under a ladder.

_____ g. After eating a chicken, people dry the collarbone, which is called the "wishbone." Two people make a wish and pull on the bone. After the bone breaks, the person holding the larger piece gets his or her wish.

UNIT 10

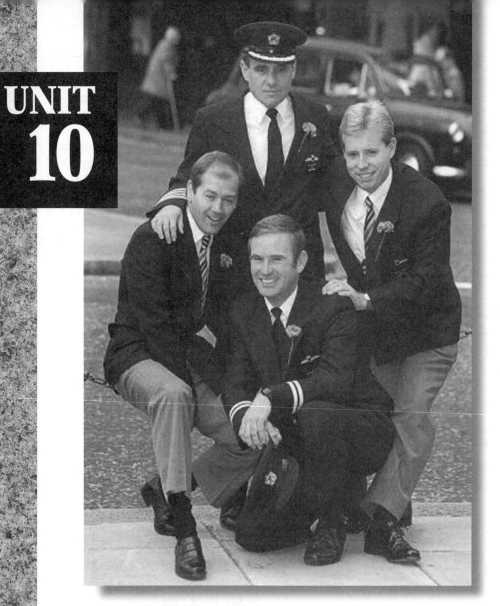

1. PRE-READING

The title of the next story is "Flight 5390." The men in the picture were the pilot, copilot, and flight attendants on Flight 5390. They are happy to be alive.

What do you think happened to Flight 5390? With a partner or in a small group, make up a story and write it down. Be sure to include:

▸ the name of the airline

▸ the month and year of the flight

▸ where the flight took off

▸ where the flight landed

▸ how many passengers were on the flight

▸ how the pilot was injured

Then read the story on the next page. Compare your story with the true story.

Flight 5390

On a beautiful June morning in 1990, Nigel Ogden stood at the door of a British Airways airplane. "Good morning! Good morning!" he said to the passengers as they boarded the plane. Nigel was a flight attendant, and he was working on a 7:30 A.M. flight from Birmingham, England, to Malaga, Spain. He was 36 years old, and he loved his job.

At 7:30, Nigel strapped himself into his seat next to Simon, another flight attendant. They talked for a few minutes about rugby,[1] Nigel's favorite sport. He not only watched the games but also played on weekends.

The plane took off, and thirteen minutes later, it was at 17,300 feet. Nigel walked into the cockpit and asked the pilot and copilot if they would like some tea. He was walking out of the cockpit when there was an enormous explosion.

Nigel turned around and saw that the pilot's windshield was completely gone, and the wind was sucking the pilot out through the window. He was already halfway out. Nigel grabbed the pilot's legs and tried to pull him back into the plane, but he couldn't; the wind was too strong. So the pilot stayed where he was—half in and half out of the plane.

The copilot was luckier; the windshield on his side was still there. He looked over at Nigel, who was holding on to the pilot's legs. "Is he OK?" he shouted over the roar of the wind. "I don't know," Nigel shouted back.

The wind was sucking everything out of the plane. Water bottles, sunglasses, hats, and books flew past Nigel's head and out the window. Nigel could feel the wind sucking him out of the plane, too. Just then Simon walked into the cockpit. He grabbed Nigel's pants belt to stop him from slipping further and strapped him into the pilot's seat. Then Simon left to take care of the passengers.

Thanks to Nigel's weekend rugby games, his arms were strong, and he was able to hold on to the pilot. But his arms were getting tired. How much longer could he hold on? He tried to see the pilot's face, but he couldn't; it was covered with blood. "We have to let him go," the copilot said. "No," Nigel said. "Maybe he's alive. I can't let him go."

While Nigel was trying to hold on to the pilot, the copilot was trying to get control of the plane. He dived down to 11,000 feet, where there was more oxygen. Then he called air-traffic control and asked for an airport with a long runway. The plane was heavy with fuel, and he was afraid it would go off the end of the runway when it landed. Air-traffic control told him that the nearest airport was in Southampton, England, and that it had only a medium-sized runway. He had to land there.

In the back of the plane, the eighty-one passengers were silent. A man with a baby on his knee said quietly, "We're going to die." "No, we aren't," Simon answered. But he thought the man was probably right.

A few minutes later, the copilot landed the plane, and it was a completely smooth landing. The plane stopped three-quarters of the way down the runway.

The passengers left the plane, and paramedics rushed in to take care of the pilot. He was covered in blood from a cut on his head, and he had a broken wrist and thumb. Otherwise, he was fine. He remembered nothing of the eighteen minutes he had been outside the plane, so he had probably been unconscious. Nigel ran out onto the front steps of the plane and shouted, "He's alive!" Then he sat down on the steps and cried.

Why had the pilot's windshield blown out? The day before, a mechanic had replaced the windshield. When he put the new windshield in, he had used bolts that were too small.

That afternoon, all but six of the passengers went on to Spain. Nigel went to see them at the departure gate. When the passengers saw Nigel, they all turned to him and applauded. Then they boarded the plane to Spain.

[1] Rugby is a sport played in Great Britain. It is similar to American football.

2. VOCABULARY

◆ LOOKING AT THE STORY

Match the words with the people, things, or actions in the picture. Write the numbers of your answers on the lines.

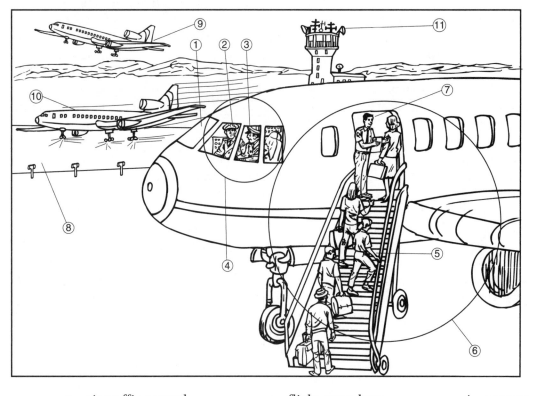

_____ a. air-traffic control

_____ b. boarding

_____ c. cockpit

_____ d. copilot

_____ e. flight attendant

_____ f. landing

_____ g. passenger

_____ h. pilot

_____ i. runway

_____ j. takeoff

_____ k. windshield

◆ LOOKING AT WORDS THAT GO TOGETHER

Some words in English go together. For example, if you ask people to complete this phrase: "*a loud* _____," most people will say "noise." The words *loud* and *noise* go together.

Ask native speakers of English to complete the following sentences and phrases, which contain words from the story. Write their answers on the lines. Then report back to the class. You and your classmates will probably have many of the same answers. When you learn these new words, learn the words that often go with them, too.

1. the *roar* of the _____

2. At the hardware store, I bought *nuts* and _____ .

3. Be careful! Don't *slip* on the _____.

4. *Strap* yourself *into* your _____.

5. The pilot made a *smooth* _____.

6. There's always a lot of traffic during *rush* _____.

3. COMPREHENSION/READING SKILLS

◆ FORMING MENTAL IMAGES AS YOU READ

Imagine this: You are going to make a movie about Flight 5390. The movie will have four scenes:

> Scene 1: At the airport in Birmingham
> Scene 2: In the cockpit of the airplane
> Scene 3: In the back of the airplane
> Scene 4: At the airport in Southampton

Read the sentences below. They describe the scenes in the movie. Some descriptions are *not* correct. Draw a line through the one incorrect description in each scene.

Scene 1: At the airport in Birmingham

▶ It is early in the morning on a sunny day.

▶ Passengers are boarding a British Airways plane.

▶ The passengers are wearing summer clothes.

▶ ~~A female flight attendant in her mid-twenties is standing at the door of the airplane.~~

Scene 2: In the cockpit

▶ The pilot's windshield is missing.

▶ The pilot is half in and half out of the airplane.

▶ A male flight attendant is sitting in the pilot's seat, holding on to the pilot's legs.

▶ Another male flight attendant is sitting in the copilot's seat. He is flying the airplane.

▶ Wind is roaring through the cockpit.

▶ Water bottles, books, and sunglasses are going out through the pilot's window.

Scene 3: In the back of the airplane

▶ There are eighty-one passengers, all strapped in their seats.

▶ Some of the passengers are screaming and crying.

▶ A flight attendant is talking to a male passenger who is holding a baby on his lap.

Scene 4: At the airport in Southampton

▶ The airplane has just landed and is at the end of the runway.

▶ Passengers are going down the stairs.

▶ Paramedics are going up the stairs.

▶ The pilot is half in and half out of the window.

◆ **UNDERSTANDING SEQUENCE**

Almost immediately after Flight 5390 landed, investigators from British Airways and the British government began trying to figure out why the pilot's windshield blew out. First, they made a time line of important events, beginning with passengers boarding at 7:00 A.M. and firefighters pulling the pilot from the plane at 8:07 A.M.

The events in the box are missing from the investigators' time line. Complete the time line by writing each event in the correct place.

Copilot calls air-traffic control; asks for emergency landing.	Passengers leave the plane; paramedics rush in.
Plane takes off.	Explosion at front of plane; pilot's windshield blows out.
Air-traffic control tells copilot to land at Southampton airport.	

7:00 A.M.   Passengers board plane.

7:30   _____

7:43   _____

7:45   Copilot dives to 11,000 feet.

7:46   _____

7:49   _____

8:01   Plane lands.

8:02   _____

8:07   Firefighters working from outside pull pilot from plane.

4. DISCUSSION

A. Which is the most dangerous way to travel—flying, driving, or taking a bus? Imagine this:

A man is traveling from Chicago, in the United States, to an island in Greece. First, he gets in his car and drives from his home to the airport in Chicago. Then he gets on a jumbo jet and flies from Chicago to Athens. In Athens, he boards a small plane to the island. After he arrives on the island, he takes a bus from the airport to his hotel.

In small groups, decide which is probably the most dangerous part of the man's trip. Tell the class your group's decision. Then look in the Answer Key to see if you were right.

B. Has anyone in your class had bad experiences flying? What happened? For example, did a plane they were on have to make an emergency landing? Did they have bad weather? Did the airline lose their luggage? Was their flight canceled?

In a small group, listen to one person's story. While you are listening, take notes in pictures (not in writing) on your own paper. Draw five to eight pictures—just enough pictures to help you remember the story. For example, here are a few of the pictures one student drew while listening to a story about changing clothes in a plane lavatory during bad weather.

After listening to the story and taking notes in pictures, practice telling the story to the people in your group. (If you forgot part of the story, you may need to add more pictures.) Then find a partner in another group. With the help of your pictures, tell your partner the story.

5. WRITING

A. With the help of your pictures, write the story you heard in Discussion Exercise B.

B. Soon after Flight 5390 landed, investigators began asking passengers and flight attendants what they saw and what they did.

Imagine that you are Nigel Ogden, a flight attendant on Flight 5390. Write a report for the investigators. In your report, tell what you saw, what you heard, and what you did. For example, you might begin:

> *At 7:00 A.M., I went to the door of the plane and greeted passengers as they boarded. Then, around 7:30, I strapped myself into my seat for takeoff. . . .*

How do you feel about flying? If you are afraid of flying, put an X on the line near the sentence "I'm afraid of flying." If you aren't afraid of flying, put an X on the line near the sentence "I'm not afraid of flying." If your feeling is somewhere in between, put an X between the two sentences.

I'm afraid of flying. ←――――――――――――――――→ I'm not afraid of flying.

Now read Part I of the Challenge reading.

 Is Flying Really Safe? ――――――――――――――――――――――

PART 1

At 3:17 on the afternoon of September 21, 2005, JetBlue Airlines Flight 292 took off from Burbank, California, and headed east toward New York City. The plane never arrived in New York. Three hours later, it landed in Los Angeles, only 7 miles from Burbank.

The problem began shortly after takeoff. The pilot noticed a warning light that indicated the landing gear was not functioning. Air-traffic controllers told the pilot to return to the airport and fly low over the control tower; maybe they could actually see what was wrong. Indeed, they could. The plane's front wheels had not gone completely up after takeoff and were stuck sideways. The controllers told the pilot to circle the plane over the Pacific Ocean to burn off its fuel and then return to California. They wanted him to land at the Los Angeles airport, which had the longest runways of all the airports in the area.

In the back of the plane, the 140 passengers on Flight 292 watched the drama on TV. JetBlue offers satellite TV on individual screens on the back of every seat, and two stations carried live coverage of the emergency. So, for three hours, the passengers watched their own news story. Some passengers appreciated having the up-to-the-minute information; others did not. "It was absolutely terrifying," one passenger said.

Four minutes before the plane landed in Los Angeles, flight attendants turned off the TVs and told the passengers to fasten their seat belts tightly and put their heads between their knees. The pilot landed the plane on its two back wheels and lowered the nose at the last minute. When the front wheels, which were still stuck sideways, hit the runway, a small fire started but went out by itself in a minute or so. It was actually a smooth landing—"the smoothest landing I ever had," one passenger said. When the plane came to a stop, the passengers clapped and cheered.

The next morning, most of the passengers boarded another JetBlue plane to New York. Martine Hughes, a 26-year-old California woman, was one of those passengers. She had always been afraid of flying, and when she boarded the second plane, she began to cry. A JetBlue flight attendant hugged her. "Everything's going to be fine," the flight attendant told her. "We'll get you to New York. This is really safe."

Has reading about JetBlue Flight 292 changed your feelings about flying? Put your X on the line again.

I'm afraid of flying. ←――――――――――――――――→ I'm not afraid of flying.

Now read Part 2 of the Challenge reading.

PART 2

When passenger Martine Hughes boarded the plane to New York, the flight attendant told her, "Everything's going to be fine. This is really safe." Was it really safe?

David Ropeik says it was. Dr. Ropeik works at Harvard University in the United States. He is an expert in risks; that is, he studies what is dangerous and what is not. Flying, he says, is not very dangerous. Why, then, are so many people afraid of flying?

Dr. Ropeik has an explanation. He says that, in general, we are afraid of risks that:

▶ we can't control.
▶ could kill us in a particularly awful way.
▶ are man-made.
▶ we often see in the news.

Flying is the type of risk that makes us fearful. That explains *why* many of us are afraid of flying. But it doesn't mean we *should* be afraid.

"We worry about the wrong things," Dr. Ropeik says, "and that's what's really dangerous." While we're busy worrying about imaginary dangers—like flying in an airplane—we're not protecting ourselves against real dangers. In the United States, someone dies in a car crash every thirteen minutes, yet 20 percent of Americans don't wear seat belts. Heart disease is the leading cause of death in the United States, yet 30 percent of Americans are obese. Lung cancer is the second leading cause of death in the United States, yet 25 percent of Americans smoke.

In the United States, flying is relatively safe: The risk of dying in a plane crash is only 1 in 3 million. Heart disease, however, is a real danger: The risk of dying of heart disease is 1 in 400. So which should we fear more—an airplane trip or the big, juicy hamburger with fries that we eat before getting on the plane? Dr. Ropeik thinks there is more danger in the hamburger than there is in the plane trip.

What would he say to Martine Hughes, the California woman who was afraid to fly to New York? "Enjoy the flight, Martine," he would say. "It really *is* safe."

Has Part 2 of the Challenge reading changed your opinion of flying? Put your X on the line again.

I'm afraid of flying. ◄——————————————————► I'm not afraid of flying.

Did the Challenge reading change your feelings about flying? Explain why or why not. Write your explanation on your own paper.

1. PRE-READING

Look at the picture and think about these questions. Discuss your answers with your classmates.

▶ Do you like stories that scare you?

▶ Do you know a scary story? Tell it to your classmates.

▶ Is your scary story true, or not true? How do you know?

A Killer in the Back Seat

Have you heard this story?

At 2:00 A.M., a young nurse left the hospital where she worked, got into her car, and headed for home. On the way home, she stopped at an all-night store for milk. As she was paying for the milk, the cashier reminded her to be careful. "You know about the murder, don't you?" he asked her.

Of course she knew about the murder. A few weeks before, a local woman who had been driving alone late at night had been murdered. The police were still looking for the killer.

The woman got into her car, locked the car doors, and pulled out of the parking lot. A man in a pickup truck pulled out right behind her and followed her, staying just inches from her rear bumper. Every few seconds, he turned on his bright lights.

Her heart pounding, the woman sped home. When she pulled into her driveway, the man in the pickup truck pulled in right behind her. The woman threw open the car door and ran toward her house. Halfway to the front door, she fainted.

When the woman came to, she saw a man kneeling beside her. He was the man in the pickup truck! "It's OK," the man said, and pointed to another man lying on the ground nearby. The man's hands and feet were tied.

"I'm the one who followed you," the stranger said. "I had just pulled into the parking lot of the all-night store when I saw a man get into your car and crouch down in the back seat. Then you came out of the store and got into the car. There was nothing I could do but follow you. I turned on my bright lights every time the guy popped up from the back seat to let him know I was behind you. When you got out of your car, he tried to run away. I hit him with my tire iron. He had a knife, but he didn't get a chance to use it. The police are on their way here. I'm sorry I scared you."

"That's all right," the woman said. "That's all right."

It is a frightening story, and it could have happened. It *could* have happened, but it didn't. It is an urban legend.

Urban legends, like ancient legends, are stories that many people tell one another. They are called "urban" legends because they often take place in or near cities.

Urban legends are not true stories. Many people believe they are true, however, because they are very realistic. In fact, sometimes urban legends are so believable, they are picked up by the news media and reported as news. If urban legends sometimes fool even experienced reporters, how can the average person know if a story is true or if it is an urban legend?

An urban legend always has this characteristic: It is a friend-of-a-friend story. Someone telling an urban legend might begin, "This really happened to my dentist's son-in-law," or "Did you hear what happened to my neighbor's cousin?" But if you try to trace the story back to the son-in-law or the cousin, the trail always evaporates.

Another characteristic of an urban legend is that it is rich in detail. An urban legend always includes the names of local people, local places, and local streets. For example, a person telling the story of the killer in the back seat would never begin, "A young nurse left the hospital where she worked." Instead, the story would begin something like this:

"You know Mr. Soto—the man who lives next door to my cousin? Well, this really happened to one of his nieces. She works at Community Hospital. Anyway, last week she was on her way home from work, about two o'clock in the morning, and . . ."

As an urban legend moves from person to person, and from city to city, the details of the story change. Mr. Soto's niece becomes Mrs. Alberti's daughter-in-law. She isn't a nurse at Community Hospital; she's a waitress at the Coffee Cup Café. The story, though, remains essentially the same, no matter how far it travels. And these days, urban legends do indeed travel far.

In the past, urban legends spread by word of mouth—one person told the story to another person. Now urban legends spread by phone and e-mail. They spread to every corner of the world, and with lightning speed.

(continued)

One final story.

This book—*Even More True Stories*—has magical powers. On the back cover of the book, there is a symbol that looks like this:

If you put your hand on the symbol and make a wish, your wish will come true. One student put her hand on the symbol and wished for a lot of money. The next day, she won the lottery—$6 million. This really happened. The student who won the lottery is the sister of my nephew's girlfriend.

2. VOCABULARY

◆ LOOKING AT THE STORY

Complete the sentences with the words in the box. Write the correct words on the lines.

came to	fool	rear bumper
detail	headed	reminded
evaporates	realistic	spread by word of mouth

1. The cashier wanted the nurse to remember that a woman had been killed.

   He _____*reminded*_____ her about the murder.

2. After the woman bought milk, she went in the direction of her house.

   She _____ for home.

3. The man in the pickup truck was behind the woman's car. He stayed just inches

   from her _____.

4. The woman fainted. A few minutes later, she woke up. When she

   _____, she saw a man kneeling beside her.

5. Urban legends are believable stories that could happen in real life. Urban legends

   are very _____.

6. The media sometimes make mistakes, and they report urban legends as news.

   Urban legends _____ even experienced reporters.

7. Someone telling an urban legend might begin, "Did you hear what happened to my

   neighbor's cousin?" But if you try to follow the story back to the cousin, the trail

   disappears. The trail _____ because the story isn't true.

8. Urban legends always include the names of local people, places, and streets; they are

   rich in _____.

9. Urban legends _____ —one person tells the story to another person.

◆ LOOKING AT SPECIAL EXPRESSIONS

Find the best way to complete each sentence. Write the letter of your answer on the line.

to pull into/onto = **to enter (while driving a car)**

<u>b</u> 1. The woman sped home and   a. pull the car into the garage.

_____ 2. It's going to rain; you'd better   b. pulled into her driveway.

_____ 3. When we got a flat tire, we   c. pulled onto the shoulder of the road.

to let someone know = **to tell someone; to inform someone**

_____ 4. The man in the pickup truck turned on his bright lights   d. please let everyone know it's at one o'clock, not two.

_____ 5. If you need any help fixing your car,   e. just let me know; I've worked as a mechanic.

_____ 6. We've changed the time of the meeting;   f. to let the man in the back seat know he saw him.

no matter how = **it makes no difference**

_____ 7. No matter how far an urban legend travels,   g. he doesn't gain weight because he exercises a lot.

_____ 8. No matter how much he eats,   h. we have to finish this job.

_____ 9. No matter how long it takes,   i. the story remains essentially the same.

3. COMPREHENSION/READING SKILLS

◆ UNDERSTANDING THE MAIN IDEAS

Check (✔) six correct ways to complete the sentence.

Urban legends . . .

_____ a. are not true.

_____ b. are ancient.

_____ c. often take place in or near cities.

_____ d. are realistic.

_____ e. are friend-of-a-friend stories.

_____ f. have many details.

_____ g. always include the names of famous people.

_____ h. remain essentially the same, no matter how far they travel.

◆ UNDERSTANDING CAUSE AND EFFECT

Find the best way to complete each sentence. Write the letter of your answer on the line.

_____ 1. Untrue stories that people tell one another are called urban legends

_____ 2. Urban legends are sometimes reported as news

_____ 3. A story that begins, "This really happened to my neighbor's cousin" might be an urban legend

_____ 4. Urban legends move from city to city, yet still include the names of local people and local places

_____ 5. These days, urban legends travel fast

a. because the storytellers change the details to fit the city.

b. because they spread not only by word of mouth, but by phone and e-mail.

c. because it has a friend-of-a-friend beginning.

d. because they are very realistic.

e. because they often take place in or near cities.

4. DISCUSSION

Below are the topics of some popular urban legends. Have you heard the stories? (If not, what do you think the stories might be?) Tell the class. (If you're curious about these urban legends, you can read many of them on the Internet. Type "urban legend" and let your search engine take you to the urban legend Web sites.)

▶ a restaurant that serves dog (or cat or rat) meat

▶ a mouse in a can of soda

▶ a young woman who is kidnapped from a dressing room in a department store (She falls through a trap door.)

▶ looking into a mirror and seeing ghosts or a woman with no eyes

▶ a poisonous snake in an imported blanket (or sweater or coat)

▶ a carpet installer who sees a bump in a carpet and finds a missing pet canary (or hamster or gerbil)

▶ a hitchhiker who disappears

▶ a female hitchhiker with hairy arms or the feet of a horse

▶ tourists in Australia who put a coat on a kangaroo

▶ a female insect that goes into someone's ear

▶ a grandmother who dies on a family vacation

▶ spiders in a cactus or yucca plant

▶ a stolen kidney

▶ stolen children

▶ a babysitter who gets a phone call from a killer

5. WRITING

Rewrite "A Killer in the Back Seat" or one of the stories your classmates told in the discussion exercise. Give the story the characteristics of an urban legend: Make it a "friend-of-a-friend" story, add details, and include the names of local people, places, and streets. This is what one student wrote.

A friend of my mom's friend is a taxi driver in São Paulo, Brazil. Her name is Monica. Like many taxi drivers, Monica has amazing stories. The story I'm going to tell you now is true. This really happened to Monica.

Monica was driving her taxi home after a long day. At exactly midnight, she was passing Primavera Cemetery and saw a woman in a black dress holding her arm out for a taxi. She stopped the taxi, and the woman got in the back seat. She introduced herself as Carol. Carol said that her car had broken down. Carol asked Monica to drive her to her parents' house on Boa Vista Street. During the whole trip, Carol asked weird questions about death. Sometimes Monica looked back at Carol just to see her face, but it was too dark and she couldn't see it. Monica also started to smell flowers in her car. It was the kind of smell that reminds you of a cemetery.

When they got to the home of Carol's parents, Carol asked Monica to wait while she went inside to get some money. Monica waited fifteen minutes. Then she went to the door and knocked three times. A man about 50 years old, wearing pajamas, answered the door. Monica said, "I'm waiting for Carol, your daughter." The man's eyes filled with tears. "Is this a bad joke?" he said. "I did have a daughter named Carol, but her funeral was at Primavera Cemetery ten years ago today. She died in a taxi accident."

Jan Harold Brunvand is a professor at the University of Utah in the United States. He has been collecting urban legends for years. Following are seven stories that Dr. Brunvand has determined are urban legends—that is, they are stories that many people believe are true but are not true. There is also one story that *is* true.

Read the eight stories. Which seven stories do you think are urban legends? Which story do you think is true?

An old woman drove her car—a Mercedes—into a crowded parking lot. She drove around for a while, looking for a parking space, and finally found one. Just as she was about to pull into the space, a young man in a shiny red sports car sped around the woman and pulled into the space. He got out of his car and smiled at the woman. "Sorry," he said. "But that's what you can do when you're young and fast."

The old woman pushed the accelerator of her Mercedes to the floor and crashed into the sports car. Then she put her car in reverse, backed up, and crashed into it again. The young man rushed over to the old woman. "What are you doing?" he yelled. The old woman handed him her insurance card and smiled. "That's what you can do when you're old and rich," she said.

During World War II, a German woman wrote a letter to relatives in the United States. In her letter, the woman said that she was fine. She suggested that her American cousin, Johnny, steam the stamp off the envelope to add to his stamp collection.

The woman's relatives were puzzled. There was no Johnny in the family, nor were there any stamp collectors. The relatives realized that this was a clue. They steamed the stamp off the envelope and found that under the stamp, the German woman had written in tiny letters: "Help us. We are starving."

Two pilots were flying an airplane with 150 passengers. The copilot left the cockpit to use the lavatory and didn't return. A long time passed. Concerned, the pilot decided to check on the copilot. He put the plane on autopilot and stepped out of the cockpit. Just then, the plane hit a pocket of turbulence, and the door to the cockpit slammed shut and locked. In order to get back into the cockpit, the two pilots had to smash the door with an ax in front of the terrified passengers.

A woman bought her boyfriend a small cell phone. She wrapped the gift and put it on a table. The next day, all that remained of the present was torn wrapping paper. The woman searched her apartment for the phone, but found nothing. She decided to dial the phone's number and heard it ringing where her dog was sleeping. At first she thought the dog was lying on the phone, but then realized that the phone was ringing *inside* the dog. She rushed the dog to the vet, who determined that the dog had indeed swallowed the phone. The vet told the woman that her dog was in no danger and told her to let nature take its course. The phone emerged from the dog the next day in perfect working order.

A woman was shopping at a large department store. She put her purse down for a minute, and it was stolen.

A few hours later, the woman was back home when the phone rang. It was a man who said he was the department store manager. He told the woman her purse was found in the store and that she could pick it up at his office.

When the woman arrived at the store, her purse was not there, and the manager knew nothing about the phone call. The woman raced home and found her keys in the lock of her front door. When she went inside, she discovered that everything of value was gone.

A young woman who lived alone had a large dog—a Doberman—for protection. One day, the woman came home from work and found the Doberman choking. The woman brought her dog to the vet.

The vet examined the dog briefly and then told the woman to go back home. The vet wanted to keep the dog for a few tests and would call the woman later.

When the woman returned home, the phone was ringing. It was the vet. "Get out of your apartment immediately!" the vet said. "Go to a neighbor's and call the police!"

The vet had found two human fingers in the Doberman's throat. When the police arrived at the woman's apartment, they found an unconscious man in a closet. The man was bleeding and missing two fingers.

A man ate some chocolate chip cookies at a small shop in a shopping mall. He liked the cookies so much that he phoned the company the next day and asked for the recipe. A company representative told the man he could not have the recipe; it was a secret. "Well," the man asked, "would you let me buy the recipe?" The representative said he could. "How much?" the man asked. "Nine-fifty," was the reply. "Just put the charge on my credit card," the man said.

When the man received his credit card statement, he found out that he had paid $950 for the chocolate chip cookie recipe. The man tried to get his money back, but he couldn't, so he decided he was going to have $950 worth of fun. He e-mailed the recipe to everyone he knew and asked them to pass it on to someone else. Now almost everyone in the country has the "secret" recipe.

A businessman was riding the New York subway home from work. The man standing next to him kept bumping into him. The businessman became suspicious and patted his back pocket. His wallet was missing! The businessman grabbed the man and shook him. "Give me the wallet!" he demanded. The man handed him a wallet.

When the businessman returned home that evening, he found his wallet on the dresser in his bedroom. The wallet in his pocket belonged to the man on the subway.

Check the Answer Key to see which story is true.

UNIT
12

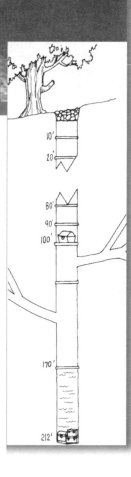

1. PRE-READING

Look at the pictures and think about these questions. Discuss your answers with your classmates.

▸ The small island in the picture is off the coast of eastern Canada. There is a deep hole on the island. Men have been digging in the hole for more than 200 years. What do you think they are trying to find?

▸ Digging in the hole is difficult. It is also dangerous: Six men have died in the hole. Look at the drawing of the hole. Can you see why digging in the hole is difficult? Can you see why it is dangerous?

The Treasure Hunt

On a summer afternoon in 1795, a teenage boy named Daniel McGinnis was exploring a tiny island off the eastern coast of Canada. He was walking through a meadow of tall grass when he noticed something strange. In the center of the meadow stood a huge oak tree with part of one branch cut off. The ground beneath that branch was lower than the surrounding ground. Daniel knew that pirates had once sailed in the waters around the island. Was this, he wondered, where they had buried their treasure?

The next day, Daniel returned to the island with shovels and two friends. The boys began digging. Two feet down, they discovered a layer of stones. Under the stones was a hole about 13 feet wide. It was filled with loose dirt. The boys kept digging for several days. Ten feet below the ground, their shovels hit an oak floor. They broke through the floor and kept digging. Twenty feet below the ground, they found another oak floor. They broke through it, too, and kept digging. But when they discovered another oak floor 30 feet below the ground, they decided that they couldn't dig any deeper. They gave up the search and left the island.

Eight years later, Daniel McGinnis, now a young man, returned with a group of men to continue digging beneath the oak tree. Day after day the men dug in the hole. One evening, 98 feet below the ground, their shovels hit a large wooden box. The box had to be a treasure chest! Certain that the treasure was almost theirs, the men went home to rest until daylight. When they returned in the morning, there was an unpleasant surprise: The hole had nearly filled with water. The men couldn't remove the water. Once again, Daniel McGinnis had to give up the search.

Over the years, other search groups came to the island. They all had the same problem: The hole filled with water. Not until 1850 did someone discover why.

In 1850, a man from a search group was eating his lunch on a beach not far from the hole. The man noticed water bubbling up through the sand. He went and got other men

from the search group. When they saw the water coming up through the sand, they, too, thought it was odd. The men decided to dig on the beach. What they found amazed them. Under the sand, there were entrances to five tunnels. All five tunnels led to the hole.

Later search groups discovered more tunnels leading from another beach to the hole. Engineers examined the tunnels. They estimated that twenty people had worked two years to build them. The tunnels were cleverly planned. If anyone digging in the hole dug deeper than 95 feet, ocean water came through the tunnels and filled the hole.

Although the water problem made digging almost impossible, more and more men came to dig on the island. The tunnels convinced them that the hole held a great treasure. None of the men found the treasure, however, and six men died trying.

In 1967, a group of investors put $3 million into a search for the treasure. They brought huge drills, pumps, and other machines to the island. After drilling 212 feet into the hole, workers sent down a video camera. The camera took pictures of three wooden chests and a human hand. But then the walls of the hole collapsed, nearly killing a worker who was in it. The investors decided that the search was too dangerous and gave it up.

Is there a pirates' treasure at the bottom of the hole? A lot of people think so. A brown, stringy material covered the oak floors that search groups found every 10 feet in the hole. That brown material came from coconut trees. Coconut trees do not grow in Canada; the nearest coconut trees are more than 800 miles away. Pirate ships could have brought the coconuts to Canada. Also, a heart-shaped stone was found in the hole. It is very similar to one that was found with pirates' treasure in the Caribbean.

If there is a pirates' treasure, it won't be easy to find. There is still the problem of water filling the hole. And there is another problem. During the past 200 years, dozens of search groups have dug in the hole, and each search group made the hole

(continued)

bigger. The hole that was once 13 feet wide is now enormous. The oak tree is gone. Where is the hole that Daniel McGinnis found? Today, nobody knows for sure, so it is impossible to know exactly where to dig.

By 2006, only two investors were still looking for the treasure. They were convinced it was somewhere in the hole, but they had to give up the search. They had been digging for forty years and were both over 80—too old to continue. They decided to put the island, including its famous hole, up for sale. The price is $5.9 million. So perhaps the treasure on the island isn't buried in the land. It is the land itself.

2. VOCABULARY

◆ LOOKING AT THE STORY

Complete the sentences with the words in the box. Write the correct words on the lines.

chest	enormous	meadow	surrounding
convinced	examining	pirates	treasure
drills	investors	shovels	

1. Daniel was walking through the tall grass of a _____*meadow*_____ when he noticed something strange.

2. The ground under the oak tree was different from the ground around it: It was lower than the _____ ground.

3. _____ once sailed near the coast of Canada, taking gold, silver, and jewels from other ships. Daniel wondered if perhaps they had buried their _____ on the island.

4. Daniel wanted to dig under the oak tree, so he returned to the island with two friends and _____.

5. When Daniel returned to the island to dig eight years later, his shovel hit a large wooden box. Was the box filled with gold and silver? Was the box a treasure _____?

6. Engineers looked at the tunnels very carefully. After _____ them, the engineers estimated that twenty people had built them.

7. When the men discovered the tunnels, they were sure that someone had buried something very important in the hole. The tunnels _____ them that the hole held a great treasure.

8. A group of people put $3 million into a search for the treasure. The

_____ hoped they would get much more than $3 million back.

9. In 1967, men brought machines to the island to help them dig. The huge

_____ dug a hole 212 feet deep.

10. Each search group made the hole bigger. The hole that was once 13 feet wide is now

_____ .

◆ LOOKING AT SPECIAL EXPRESSIONS

Find the best way to complete each sentence. Write the letter of your answer on the line.

to give up = **to stop working at; to stop trying**

_____ 1. The boys decided that they couldn't dig any deeper and

a. but I hurt my leg and had to give up running.

_____ 2. I used to run a mile a day,

b. gave up their search.

_____ 3. He tried to call his mother yesterday, but the line was busy;

c. he dialed her number for twenty minutes and then gave up.

3. COMPREHENSION/READING SKILLS

◆ UNDERSTANDING TIME RELATIONSHIPS

Check (✔) three correct ways to complete each sentence.

1. Before 1795,
   _____ a. a deep hole was dug on an island.
   _____ b. tunnels were built from the beach to the hole.
   _____ c. the walls of the hole collapsed.
   _____ d. pirates sailed in the waters off the eastern coast of Canada.

2. In 1795,
   _____ a. Daniel McGinnis discovered an oak tree with part of one branch cut off.
   _____ b. Daniel McGinnis and two friends dug under the oak tree.
   _____ c. investors raised lots of money to search for the treasure.
   _____ d. oak floors were found 10, 20, and 30 feet below the ground.

3. Eight years after Daniel McGinnis discovered the hole,
   _____ a. he returned with a group of men to continue digging.
   _____ b. men digging 98 feet down hit a wooden object with their shovels.
   _____ c. the hole filled with water.
   _____ d. six men died trying to find the treasure.

(continued)

4. In 1850,

    _____ a. a man from a search group ate his lunch on a beach not far from the hole.

    _____ b. investors brought huge drills, pumps, and other machines to the island.

    _____ c. a search group saw water coming up through the sand.

    _____ d. men found tunnels that led from a beach to the hole.

5. In 1967,

    _____ a. a group of investors put $3 million into a search for the treasure.

    _____ b. workers drilled 212 feet and then sent down a video camera.

    _____ c. workers discovered a layer of stones in the hole.

    _____ d. the walls of the hole collapsed, nearly killing a worker who was in it.

◆ **SCANNING FOR INFORMATION**

The underlined information is incorrect. Find the correct information in the story and write it. Work quickly; try to complete this exercise in three minutes or less.

1. In 1795, a teenage boy named Daniel <u>McDonald</u> *McGinnis* was exploring a tiny island off the eastern coast of Canada.

2. In the center of the meadow stood a huge <u>maple</u> tree with part of one branch cut off.

3. <u>Two days later</u>, Daniel returned to the island with shovels and two friends.

4. <u>Three</u> feet down, they discovered a layer of stones.

5. Under the stones was a hole about <u>12</u> feet wide.

6. <u>Ten</u> years later, Daniel, now a young man, returned with a group of men to continue digging beneath the oak tree.

7. One <u>afternoon</u>, 98 feet below the ground, their shovels hit a large wooden box.

8. In <u>1860</u>, a man from a search group was eating his lunch on a beach near the hole.

9. Under the sand, the man found entrances to <u>four</u> tunnels.

10. Engineers estimate that <u>forty</u> people worked two years to build them.

4. DISCUSSION

A. Talk about the hole. First answer the questions by circling *Yes* or *No*.

1. The hole, with its oak floors and water tunnels, is complicated. Many people say that no group of pirates could have dug the hole. What do you think? Did pirates dig the hole?   YES   NO

2. The last two investors still believe there is a great treasure in the hole. Do you think there is a great treasure in the hole?   YES   NO

3. Would you like to go to the island and dig for the treasure?   YES   NO

4. If you were very rich, would you buy the island?   YES   NO

Now work as a class and answer these questions.

5. How many students think that pirates dug the hole? (If the pirates didn't dig the hole, then who did?)

6. How many students think there is a great treasure in the hole? What do they think the treasure is? How much do they think it's worth? (Some people say, "Billions of dollars." Is that possible?)

7. How many students would like to go to the island and dig for the treasure? Why do those students want to go there? Why do some students not want to go there?

8. How many students would buy the island if they were rich? What would they do with it? (Here are some ideas: Continue to look for the treasure; make the island a tourist attraction; build luxury homes there.)

B. Talk about other treasures. Think about these questions and discuss your answers with your classmates.

1. Has a great treasure ever been discovered in your native country? What was the treasure? Who buried it? Who discovered it? What happened to it?

2. Do you know about any other searches for treasure? What were the searchers looking for? What did they find?

5. WRITING

One of the investors who put $3 million into a search said, "This could be one of the greatest treasures ever found."

What is your greatest treasure? Write about it. Here is what one student wrote.

My greatest treasure is my mother.

When I was little, I often had bad dreams. When I woke up, my mother always held me and took me into the garden for a short time. Then I could fall back to sleep again.

My mother always told me that I was not like other little girls. She told me I was special. Maybe that was true, and maybe it wasn't. But my mother believed it was true.

Sometimes I try to imagine that I am not my mother's daughter but someone else's daughter. I can't imagine it. I can't imagine having a different mother. She is my greatest treasure.

In 1795, Daniel McGinnis began looking for treasure on Oak Island. More than 200 years later, people are still searching for the treasure. There is another treasure that people have been trying to find for a long time. It is Beale's treasure, which—if it exists—is buried in the United States, somewhere in Virginia. People have been looking for that treasure for more than 150 years.

Read the story of Beale's treasure.

 Thomas Beale's Treasure

In 1817, thirty men, led by Thomas Beale, left their homes in Virginia to hunt in Colorado. One evening, while camping in a canyon, one of the men spotted gold in nearby rocks. The men immediately gave up hunting and began mining the gold. Later, they discovered silver in the same area. Working almost constantly for eighteen months, they accumulated a great treasure—1,000 pounds of gold and 2,000 pounds of silver. Worried that their treasure would be stolen, the men decided that Thomas Beale and ten of the men would transport it back to Virginia. Beale and the men would hide the treasure there and then return to the mine. The men gave Thomas Beale a second task: They told him to find a reliable man in Virginia, someone who would distribute the treasure to their families if they did not return from Colorado.

While he was in Virginia looking for a place to hide the treasure, Beale stayed at a small hotel owned by man named Robert Morriss. Robert Morriss was an honest man, well liked by his neighbors. In the two months he stayed at Morriss's hotel, Beale got to know Morriss quite well. When Beale returned to the mine in Colorado, he recommended Morriss as a man who could be trusted with the secret of the treasure. The men approved Beale's choice.

Two years later, Beale returned to Virginia to hide another wagonload of gold and silver. Again, he stayed at Morriss's hotel. Before he went back to Colorado the third time, Beale gave Morriss an iron box to keep for him. He told Morriss to open the box if he did not come back within ten years.

Beale never returned. Morriss left the box untouched for more than twenty years. In 1845, he decided that Beale had probably died, and he opened the iron box. What was in the box? There was a letter from Beale. In his letter, Beale told Morriss about the discovery of gold and silver in Colorado. He also told Morriss that in the box he would find three ciphers—information written in a secret code. The ciphers, Beale wrote, would lead Morriss to a great treasure. The first cipher revealed the location of the treasure; the second cipher described the treasure; and the third cipher listed the relatives of all thirty men. After he found the treasure, Morriss was to divide it into thirty-one parts. Thirty parts were for the families of the men who had mined the treasure in Colorado, and one part was for Morriss to keep.

Morriss looked at the ciphers. They consisted of rows and rows of numbers—more than 500 numbers in each cipher. In his letter, Beale said that he would mail Morriss a decoding key—a paper that would tell Morriss what the numbers in the ciphers stood for. But in the twenty years that Morriss had kept the box, no key had ever arrived. Morriss knew that it was up to him to decode the ciphers.

Morriss never succeeded in decoding the ciphers, although he spent the rest of his life trying. Before he died in 1863, he told a friend, James Ward, about the treasure and gave him the ciphers. After years of work, Ward was able to decode cipher 2, which described the treasure. He discovered that the code in cipher 2 was based on a U.S. document—the Declaration of Independence. Beale had given the first letter of each word in the Declaration of Independence a number:

1   2   3   4   5   6   7
When in the course of human events,
8 9   10   11
it becomes necessary for . . .

Now all Ward had to do was match the letters in the Declaration of Independence with the numbers in the cipher. The message began:

"I have deposited in the county of Bedford, Virginia, about 4 miles from Buford's Tavern, in a vault 6 feet below the ground, 2,921 pounds of gold and 5,100 pounds of silver, and jewels valued at $13,000."

After he decoded cipher 2, Ward knew *what* the treasure was. But to know *where* it was, he had to decode cipher 1. For the next thirty years, he became obsessed with decoding it. He neglected his family, his friends, and his business. Ultimately, he went broke and had to give up. Since he had no hope of decoding cipher 1 himself, Ward decided to share it with the world. In 1894, he published a twenty-three-page booklet, *The Beale Papers*. In the booklet, Ward recounted the history of the ciphers and printed all three of them.

Since the publication of *The Beale Papers*, people have spent countless hours trying to decode the ciphers—especially cipher 1, which tells where the treasure is buried. Many people find that once they start working on the ciphers, it is difficult to stop. They, like Ward, become obsessed with finding solutions. There is even a club—The Beale Cypher Association—for people who are dedicated to decoding the ciphers. Anyone who joins the association receives the results of the members' work so far.

Experts who have examined the ciphers believe that they are real and have solutions. Because cipher 2 was based on a document, it seems likely that ciphers 1 and 3 are based on old documents, too. Lately, most people are using computers to try to decode the ciphers. They are scanning old documents into computers and letting the computers give numbers to the letters in the documents. So far, even the computers have been unable to decode the ciphers.

Although the ciphers are certainly real, is the treasure real? Did Beale bury gold, silver, and jewels somewhere in Virginia, about four miles from Buford's Tavern? Of course, people have dug in the area. They found nothing. Perhaps the story is a hoax. Perhaps Thomas Beale made up the whole story and passed it on to Robert Morriss. Or perhaps Robert Morriss made up the whole story and passed it on to Robert Ward. Or perhaps Robert Ward made up the whole story and passed it on to the world.

It is not certain that Beale's treasure exists, yet people keep trying to decode the ciphers. Why do they continue to try? For one thing, the challenge of finding solutions to the puzzles is compelling. Some people simply want to accomplish something people have been trying to do for more than 100 years. And there is another reason to persist: If Thomas Beale really did bury 8,000 pounds of gold and silver somewhere in Virginia, the treasure is worth more than $20 million today.

Now discuss these questions.

▸ Which search—the search for treasure on Oak Island or the search for Beale's treasure—do you think might be successful?

▸ If you had the time and money to search for treasure, which treasure would you try to find?

1. PRE-READING

Look at the picture and guess the answers to these questions.

▶ In what country was the picture taken?

▶ In what year was the picture taken?

Listen while your classmates tell their guesses. Then look in the Answer Key for the correct answers. Did the answers surprise you? Do you know anything about the Amish? If you do, tell the class what you know.

The Plain People

It is still dark when Elizabeth wakes up. She gets out of bed and shivers when her feet touch the cold, bare floor. The bedroom is not heated, and it is so cold that she can see her breath. She quickly puts on her long dress, black apron, and black shoes. Then she hurries downstairs to the kitchen.

The only light in the kitchen comes from kerosene lamps; Elizabeth's husband lit the lamps earlier, before he went out to milk the cows. Elizabeth puts a few pieces of wood into the stove and starts the fire. Then she begins to prepare a big breakfast for herself, her husband, and their six children. It is the beginning of a typical day for Elizabeth.

Although Elizabeth's day will be typical, her life is certainly not typical of modern life in the United States. Elizabeth belongs to a religious group known as the Amish. The Amish are often called "the plain people" because they live and dress very simply. Their homes have no carpets on the floors, no pictures on the walls, and no soft, comfortable furniture. The men wear dark pants with white or blue shirts, and the women wear long dresses in dark colors. The women never wear makeup or jewelry.

The Amish have a saying: "The old way is the best way." Although the Amish accept some new ideas—they use new medicines, for example—their way of life has not changed much in 300 years. They do not use electricity, so Amish homes have no electric lights, no TVs, and no kitchen appliances like refrigerators. The Amish don't own telephones, either. They ride in buggies pulled by horses, and when they speak to one another, they speak German, the language that the first Amish people spoke.

The first Amish people lived in Germany and Switzerland. They were called Amish because their leader was Jacob Amman. The Amish were persecuted in Europe, so around 1720, they came to the New World. They settled in what is now the state of Pennsylvania.

Most of the Amish still live in Pennsylvania, although there are large communities in other states, too. All Amish, no matter where they live, have similar beliefs.

The Amish believe that life in the countryside is best, so many Amish live on farms. Amish farmers do not use modern machinery, yet their farms are successful because the Amish work hard and take good care of their land and animals. Their farms are always small. The Amish think it is wrong to have more land or more money than they need to live. About twenty years ago, some Amish farmers discovered oil on their land. Was there a lot of oil under the ground, or just a little? The Amish farmers didn't want to know. They immediately sold their land and moved away, without telling anyone about the oil. They didn't want to be rich.

The Amish, who are Christians, believe they should follow the peaceful example of Jesus. Amish men will not fight in wars or serve in the army. They will not even wear coats with buttons, because military uniforms often have large gold or silver buttons.

The Amish will not buy insurance of any kind. When there is trouble, they help one another. If an Amish farmer gets sick, relatives and neighbors will milk his cows, plant his fields, and harvest his crops. If a barn burns down, as many as 200 men will come and build a new barn in one day.

The Amish are not allowed to marry people who are not Amish. That has caused a peculiar problem. The 500 or so Amish who came to the New World in the 1700s had about forty last names. The 200,000 Amish who live in the United States today are the descendants of those people—and have the same forty last names. In one school in Pennsylvania, 95 percent of the students—and their teacher—have the last name "Stolzfus." The Amish custom of choosing first names from the Bible adds to the problem. In one small Amish community, there are eleven men named Daniel Miller!

To avoid confusion, the Amish give nicknames to people who have the same name. Some nicknames have an obvious explanation: "Chicken Dan" sells chickens,

(continued)

for example; "Curly Dan" has curly hair. But what about "Gravy Dan"? How did he get his nickname? At dinner one evening, this Dan wanted to pour some cream into his coffee. He reached for the pitcher of cream but took the pitcher of gravy by mistake, and poured gravy into his coffee. Ever since that evening, his nickname has been "Gravy Dan."

People are curious about the lives of Amish like Elizabeth and Gravy Dan. Every year thousands of tourists visit the part of Pennsylvania where most Amish live. They take pictures of the black buggies and the plain white houses. They watch Amish children as they walk to school and Amish men as they work in their fields. Most Amish are not happy about the tourists, but they tolerate them. Perhaps the Amish understand that the tourists want to experience—at least for a few days—the quieter, simpler Amish way of life.

2. VOCABULARY

◆ LOOKING AT THE STORY

Read each sentence. What is the meaning of the word(s) in italics? Circle the letter of the correct answer.

1. Elizabeth shivers when her feet touch the cold, *bare* floor.
   a. not covered with a carpet
   b. painted white

2. They do not use electricity, so Amish people have no kitchen *appliances* like refrigerators.
   a. machines run by electricity and used in the house
   b. furniture made out of wood and used in the house

3. The Amish *were persecuted* in Europe, so they came to the New World.
   a. People were cruel to them.
   b. People were friendly to them.

4. They *settled* in what is now the state of Pennsylvania.
   a. found a new leader
   b. came to live

5. There are large Amish *communities* in other states, too.
   a. groups of people who left their countries because of politics
   b. groups of people who live together

6. All Amish have similar *beliefs*.
   a. objects that are important to them
   b. ideas that they think are true

7. Amish men will not fight in wars. They will not even wear coats with buttons because *military uniforms* often have large gold or silver buttons.
   a. the clothes worn by schoolchildren
   b. the clothes worn by soldiers

8. If an Amish farmer gets sick, relatives and neighbors will *harvest his crops*.
   a. pick the fruit, vegetables, and grain that he grows
   b. bring him the medicine and other things that he needs

9. If a *barn* burns down, as many as 200 men will come and build a new barn in one day.
   a. house that is made of wood and built by hand
   b. building where a farmer keeps his crops and animals

10. The Amish are not allowed to marry people who are not Amish. That has caused a *peculiar* problem.
    a. big   b. strange

11. A man took a pitcher of *gravy* by mistake and poured it into his coffee.
    a. drink made with lemons and sugar   b. sauce for meat and potatoes

12. Most Amish are not happy about the tourists, but they *tolerate them*.
    a. allow them to come   b. make them pay

◆ LOOKING AT A NEW CONTEXT

Complete the sentences to show that you understand the meanings of the new words. Then in small groups, take turns reading your sentences aloud. Ask your classmates questions about their sentences.

1. A new kitchen appliance that my family really needs is a(n) _____.

2. A modern-day example of people who are persecuted is _____.

3. If I had to leave my native country, I would settle in _____.

4. A strong belief I have is that _____.

5. Some crops that are harvested near my native city are _____.

6. Something I could never tolerate is _____.

3. COMPREHENSION/READING SKILLS

◆ UNDERSTANDING THE MAIN IDEAS

What information is *not* in the story? Draw a line through the information.

1. Elizabeth _____.
   a. sleeps in a bedroom that is not heated
   b. wears a long dress, black apron, and black shoes
   c. ~~has two sons~~
   d. cooks on a wood stove

2. The Amish _____.
   a. are a religious group also called "the plain people"
   b. live and dress very simply
   c. live in California
   d. believe that "the old way is the best way"

3. The first Amish people _____.
   a. spoke French
   b. were led by Jacob Amman
   c. were persecuted in Europe
   d. came to the New World around 1720

(continued)

4. Some Amish beliefs are: _____.
   a. Life in the countryside is best
   b. Follow the peaceful example of Jesus
   c. Do not buy insurance
   d. Do not work on Mondays

◆ UNDERSTANDING SUPPORTING DETAILS

Find the best way to complete each sentence. Write the letter of your answer on the line.

_____ 1. Elizabeth's life is not typical of life in the United States in the twenty-first century. For example,

_____ 2. The Amish dress very simply. For example,

_____ 3. The Amish way of life has not changed much in 300 years. For example,

_____ 4. The Amish help one another when there is trouble. For example,

_____ 5. Some nicknames have an obvious explanation. For example,

a. they still speak German, the language that the first Amish people spoke.

b. "Chicken Dan" sells chickens and "Curly Dan" has curly hair.

c. she cooks on a wood stove.

d. if a barn burns down, as many as 200 men will come and build a new barn in a day.

e. the women wear long dresses in dark colors.

4. DISCUSSION

A. Think about these questions. Discuss your answers with your classmates.

1. Amish life is not typical of life in the United States. Are there any small religious groups in your native country who live differently from most people in your country? Tell your classmates about them.

2. Could you live the way the Amish live? Could you live without electricity, without a car, and without a telephone? Explain why or why not.

3. Some Amish beliefs include the following:
   ▶ It is wrong to have more money than you need.
   ▶ Never fight in wars.
   ▶ Help one another when there is trouble.
   What do you think about these beliefs? Do you agree with them?

4. There is confusion because many Amish have the same last name. Are there some last names that are very common in your native country? What are the names?

5. The Amish give one another nicknames. Do you have a nickname? What is it? Is there a story behind your nickname, like the story of "Gravy Dan"? If you would like, share it with your classmates.

B. Think about a religion you know and answer the questions in the chart. Then ask a partner the questions and write your partner's answers in the chart.

	You	Your Partner
1. Which religion do you know the most about?		
2. Where does this religion get its name?		
3. Does this religion have many different groups? If so, what are some of them called?		
4. Is there a holy book? What is it called?		
5. Is any day of the week special? Which day? What do people do on that day?		
6. Which religious holiday is most important? What does the holiday celebrate? What do people do on that holiday?		
7. Are there any rules about food?		
8. Are there any rules about clothing?		
9. What does this religion say happens to people after they die?		

5. WRITING

Write about one of the world's religions. Use the information you wrote in Exercise 4B, or use the information your partner gave you. Here is what one student wrote.

The Mormon religion is a Christian religion that began about 175 years ago. Most Mormons live in the United States, in the state of Utah.

Mormons have a lot of rules. They don't drink alcohol. They also don't drink coffee, tea, cola, or any drink that has caffeine in it. They must pay the church 10 percent of their income.

In the Mormon church, there are no paid priests or ministers. People volunteer to work as ministers.

Years ago, Mormon men had more than one wife. The Mormons' neighbors and the U.S. government didn't like that, and there was a lot of trouble. But today, Mormon men have just one wife.

Following are five paragraphs that give more information about Amish life. On page 111, there are five photos.

Read the paragraphs. Then match each paragraph with the photo that fits it best. Write the number of the paragraph below the photo. Be sure to read each paragraph to the end before you make your choice.

1 When Amish boys are 16, they are given special buggies—called courting buggies—so that they can give girls rides. Some boys add carpeting to their buggies and install stereos. This is actually against the Amish practice of being plain, but adults tolerate it. Some boys even add speedometers so they can see if their buggies can go faster than the average speed of a buggy, which is about 12 miles per hour. One Amish man said, "If you clock a buggy going 15 miles an hour, you can be sure it's a teenage driver!" It is easy to tell a courting buggy from a regular buggy. A regular buggy is covered and looks like a box sitting on wheels, but a courting buggy is open, with no roof.

2 The Amish have a saying: "The more you learn, the more you are confused." The Amish believe that education after the eighth grade— that is, after a child is 13 or 14—is unnecessary. That belief caused a serious problem for the Amish in the 1960s. Some states began enforcing laws that required school attendance until age 16, and Amish teenagers had to go to high school. In some cases, police forced Amish children onto school buses while their parents stood by, crying and praying. The Amish did nothing to change the law because they believe that any type of protest—even filing a lawsuit—is wrong. Many non-Amish, however, wanted to help. They formed a group called the National Committee for Amish Religious Freedom, and filed a lawsuit. The case was decided by the U.S. Supreme Court in 1972. The court ruled unanimously that Amish children were exempt from the law and could leave school after the eighth grade. So, today, Amish children are educated in the same way their parents and grandparents were educated—by Amish teachers in one-room schoolhouses. Their formal education stops after eight years.

3 Amish families gather every other Sunday for a worship service that lasts four hours. At an Amish service, the men and women sit separately on wooden benches, and the children sit on benches at the back of the room. (Halfway through the service, the children are given a snack to help them make it to the next meal.) When the service is over, the benches are removed and tables are set up for lunch. The meal is simple but plentiful: There are sandwiches and soup; pickles and pickled beets; bread, butter, and jam; and pies and cake for dessert. Amish services, as well as the meal that follows them, take place not in church buildings— the Amish have no churches—but in people's homes. Anyone on a Sunday drive through the Amish countryside easily can tell where the Sunday services are being held: There will be twenty to thirty-five buggies parked outside the house.

4 The Amish are one of the fastest-growing religious groups in the United States because Amish families have so many children. The average number of children in an Amish family is six, but families with eleven or twelve children are not uncommon. Their growing population has caused a hard-to-solve problem for the Amish. Farmland has become expensive in the United States, and most Amish cannot afford to buy it. As a result, the Amish have too little land for too many people. Some Amish have turned to professions other than farming, with furniture-making being the most popular. Amish-made furniture, which is sold in stores all over the United States, is prized for its quality and durability.

5 In 1985, the movie *Witness* was filmed in Lancaster, Pennsylvania, the home of many Amish. The movie tells the story of an Amish widow who falls in love with a police detective from Philadelphia, played by Harrison Ford. The movie was made without the permission of the Amish, who opposed the film. One scene in the movie particularly offended the Amish. Harrison Ford, dressed in plain clothes, defends his Amish friends in a fistfight. That scene was filmed in front of Zimmerman's Hardware Store, where Amish actually shop. Later, laws were passed in Pennsylvania to protect the Amish from similar movies being made without their permission.

a. _____

b. _____

c. _____

d. _____

e. _____

UNIT 14

1. PRE-READING

Think about these questions. Discuss your answers with your classmates.

▶ Do you know of any old person who died soon after an important event, like a holiday or birthday?

▶ Do you think that people can control the time of their own deaths?

Does Death Take a Holiday?

Yinlan looked at the people sitting around the table and smiled contentedly. Everyone in her family was there—her children, her grandchildren, and her new great-grandson, just 1 month old. Her whole family had come to celebrate the Harvest Moon Festival.

The Harvest Moon Festival is a Chinese celebration. Although Yinlan no longer lived in China—she lived in San Francisco—she and her family still celebrated the Harvest Moon Festival just as Yinlan had in China. At the time of the full moon in August or September, her family gathered at her house for dinner. After dinner, they ate moon cakes, a special round cookie. Then, if the sky was clear, they always walked outside to admire the full moon.

Tonight, there was not a cloud in the sky, and the full moon shone brightly. Yinlan suggested that they all go outside. Her grandson helped her up from her chair. As Yinlan and her grandson walked toward the door, she held on to his arm and leaned against him for support. Yinlan was 86 years old. She had not been well the past few months, and her family noticed that she seemed weak.

Two days after the Harvest Moon Festival, Yinlan died peacefully in her sleep. Her family was sad but at the same time grateful. They felt happy that they had been able to celebrate the Harvest Moon Festival with her one last time. They said it seemed that she had waited until after the holiday to die.

Had she waited? Is it possible for people to postpone the time of their deaths? Sociologists have been trying to answer that question for many years. In 1990, a sociologist studied the death rate among elderly Chinese women in California from 1960 to 1984. He discovered that the death rate dropped before the Harvest Moon Festival and then rose: Each year there were fewer deaths than usual the week before the festival, and more deaths than usual the week after. The sociologist believed that these changes in the death rate showed the mind's power over the body. The Harvest Moon Festival, when families gather, is important to elderly Chinese women. Apparently some women were able to postpone their deaths so that they could celebrate the festival one last time. But then, in 2004, another researcher studied the death rate among elderly Chinese women in California during a different time period, from 1985 to 2000. During those years, there were about the same number of deaths before and after the festival. That researcher concluded that Chinese women did not postpone their deaths until after the Harvest Moon Festival.

Sociologists also studied the death rate of elderly Jewish men around the time of Passover. Passover is a Jewish religious holiday that is a family holiday as well. On the first two days of Passover, families gather in their homes for a ceremony. They sit around a table to share a special meal and to listen to the story of Passover. Traditionally, the oldest man in the family sits at the head of the table and reads the story. It is an important event for elderly Jewish men. Sociologists wondered if some Jewish men postponed their deaths until after Passover.

To find out, they studied the death rate among elderly Jewish men in several parts of the world. They discovered that in Connecticut, the death rate dropped before Passover and then rose. That fact seemed to show that Jewish men waited until after Passover to die. But in Israel, the death rate did not change around the holiday, and in California, the death rate actually rose before Passover and then dropped.

The idea that people can postpone the time of their deaths is not new. Many families tell stories of a relative who held on to life until after an important event. They tell of a grandmother who died after the birth of a grandchild, a grandfather who died after his 92nd birthday party. Historians tell stories, too, about famous people like Thomas Jefferson. Jefferson wrote the Declaration of Independence, one of the most important U.S. documents. The Declaration of Independence was signed on July 4, 1776. Jefferson died exactly fifty years later, on July 4, 1826. He died after asking his doctor, "Is it the Fourth?"

(continued)

All these stories, however, are just that: stories. They are not proof that people can postpone their deaths. The sociologists are studying death rates because death rates are facts, not stories. Only facts can prove that people really can postpone their deaths. So far, the facts haven't proven it.

Still, many nurses and social workers who work with dying people are convinced that people can postpone their deaths, at least for a few days. "We don't know how people stay alive," one social worker says, "and I don't think we'll ever really know, but sometimes they do. We cannot measure the human spirit."

2. VOCABULARY

◆ LOOKING AT THE STORY

Read each sentence. Which word or phrase below has the same meaning as the word(s) in italics? Write the letter of your answer on the line.

_f_ 1. Yinlan was an *old* Chinese woman.

_____ 2. She celebrated the Harvest Moon Festival *exactly* as she had in China.

_____ 3. Her family *came together* for a special dinner.

_____ 4. She looked at the people sitting around the table and smiled *happily*.

_____ 5. When Yinlan died, her family was sad but also *thankful*.

_____ 6. Sociologists wondered if elderly Chinese women *waited* until after the Harvest Moon Festival *to die*.

_____ 7. They studied the *number of deaths* among Chinese women around the time of the festival.

_____ 8. During one time period, the death rate *went down* before the festival.

_____ 9. Then it *went up* after the festival.

_____ 10. *It seemed that* some Chinese women were able to postpone their deaths.

_____ 11. A researcher who studied the death rate during a different time period *looked at the information and decided* that Chinese women did not postpone their deaths until after the holiday.

_____ 12. Thomas Jefferson, who wrote an important U.S. *paper*, may have postponed his death.

_____ 13. Many nurses and social workers are *sure* that people can postpone their deaths.

---

a. grateful

b. rose

c. postponed their deaths

d. contentedly

e. convinced

f. elderly

g. gathered

h. just

i. dropped

j. concluded

k. apparently

l. document

m. death rate

Answer the questions to show that you understand the meanings of the new words. (You don't need to write complete sentences.) Then in small groups, take turns sharing your answers.

1. When was the last time your family gathered for a celebration?

   _____

2. Name someone or something you are grateful for. _____

3. Who is an elderly person that you admire? _____

4. What would a visitor to your country probably conclude about the people who live there?

   _____

5. Name something you would like to postpone. _____

6. What is an important document in your country? _____

7. What usually convinces you that something is true? _____

3. COMPREHENSION/READING SKILLS

◆ **UNDERSTANDING A SUMMARY**

Following is a summary of the information in "Does Death Take a Holiday?" Complete the summary. Write your answers on the lines.

Sociologists want to know if people can _____*postpone*_____ the time of
                                            1.
their _____. To find out, they have been studying death
            2.
_____ around the time of holidays. For example, they studied the
         3.
death rate of _____ women in California around the time of the
                    4.
Harvest _____ Festival. During the time period from 1960
              5.
to 1984, the death rate _____ before the festival and
                              6.
_____ after it. But during the years 1985–2000, there were the
         7.
_____ number of deaths before and after the festival.
      8.

Families tell stories of a _____ who held on to life until after an
                                  9.
_____ event. But the stories are not _____ that
      10.   11.
people can postpone their deaths. Sociologists are studying death rates because death

rates are _____, not stories. So far, the death rates have not proven
                 12.
that people can postpone their deaths.

◆ SCANNING FOR INFORMATION

The underlined information is incorrect. Find the correct information in the story and write it. Work quickly; try to complete this exercise in three minutes or less.

1. Yinlan was <u>88</u> years old. *86*

2. She died <u>five</u> days after the Harvest Moon Festival.

3. Sociologists studied the death rate among elderly Chinese women in <u>Florida</u>.

4. They also studied the death rate of elderly Jewish men at the time of <u>Hanukkah</u>, a Jewish holiday.

5. On the first <u>three</u> days of Passover, families gather in their homes for a ceremony.

6. In <u>Massachusetts</u>, the death rate dropped before Passover and rose after it.

7. But in <u>Russia</u>, the death rate did not change, and in California, it actually rose before Passover and dropped after it.

8. Historians tell stories about famous people like <u>William</u> Jefferson.

9. Jefferson was the author of the <u>Bill of Rights</u>, one of the most important U.S. documents.

10. The Declaration of Independence was signed on July 4, <u>1774</u>.

11. Jefferson died exactly <u>forty</u> years later.

12. Many nurses and social workers who work with dying people are convinced that people can postpone their deaths, at least for a few <u>weeks</u>.

4. DISCUSSION

Think about these questions. Discuss your answers with your classmates.

1. One question in the pre-reading exercise was: "Do you think that people can control the time of their own deaths?" After reading the story, is your answer to that question still the same, or has it changed?

2. Do you think the mind has power over the body? Do you think, for example, that people can control whether or not they get sick or feel pain?

3. The Harvest Moon Festival is important to elderly Chinese women because their families gather for a special meal. Passover is important to elderly Jewish men because they sit at the head of the table and tell the story of Passover. Which holiday is important to the elderly people in your family? Why is it important to them?

4. Thomas Jefferson died on July 4, 1826, exactly fifty years after the Declaration of Independence was signed. Do you think it was just a coincidence? Or do you think Jefferson postponed his death until the Fourth of July?

5. WRITING

A. The sociologists believe that their studies show the mind's power over the body. Have you ever used your mind to control your body? Do you know a story that shows that the mind can control the body? Write a paragraph or two. Here is what one student wrote.

> I read a story in the newspaper about an elderly woman who was dying in a hospital. She asked the doctor to call her only son because she wanted to see him one last time. But before her son arrived, the woman's heart stopped beating. The doctor met the woman's son in the lobby of the hospital and told him that his mother had died. When the son went to his mother's room and began to cry, a machine connected to the woman showed that the woman's heart was beating again. The woman opened her eyes, looked at her son, and smiled. A few minutes later, she peacefully left the world again.

B. Write about a holiday that is important to you. How do you celebrate it? Here is what one student wrote.

> When I was a little girl, my favorite day was March 3. That is when people in Japan celebrate Hinamatsuri, a holiday for girls. The girls dress dolls in beautiful dresses called kimonos and display the dolls. Girls usually get the dolls ready about a week before the holiday. (People say that girls who dress their dolls early get married early, but that wasn't true for me! I always dressed my dolls early, but I am 26 years old and not married.) The first time a girl celebrates Hinamatsuri, her relatives come to her house. Everybody drinks "Shirozake," a special drink, and eats sweets we call "Sakuramochi." The next day, on March 4, the girls put their dolls away. I always felt a little sad when Hinamatsuri was over and it was time to put my dolls away.

Imagine this: You have a friend—let's say his name is Sam—who is afraid of taking tests. Sam always studies hard but often panics when he takes an exam. His mind goes blank, and he can't remember anything. Next week, Sam has a big exam. He's going to study for the exam, of course, but he's also going to prepare for the exam using guided imagery. For fifteen minutes every day, he's going to imagine himself taking the exam. He's going to close his eyes and see himself walking into the classroom. He's going to feel the pencil in his hand and see the exam on his desk. He's going to imagine feeling calm and confident as he writes the answers.

Do you think this preparation will help Sam? Circle the letter of your answer.

    a. Yes, definitely   c. Maybe   e. Definitely not

    b. Probably   d. Probably not

Now read Part 1.

 Mind Over Matter?

PART 1

Many people believe that the mind has so much power over the body that people can postpone the time of their deaths. So far, sociologists have not been able to prove that this is true. Still, most researchers do not deny that there is a connection between the mind and the body. If you'd like to experience the mind-body connection yourself, do this simple experiment:

Imagine that you are standing in the kitchen. Take a few minutes to look around the kitchen you see in your mind. Notice the color of the kitchen table, appliances, and cupboards. Notice, too, any kitchen sounds, like the hum of the refrigerator. Notice any smells. Now imagine that a cutting board is in front of you. Next to it is a sharp knife.

Next, imagine that on the cutting board there is a plump, fresh, juicy lemon. In your mind, hold the lemon in one hand. Then put it back on the board. Carefully cut it in half with the knife. Now look at the two halves of the lemon. Notice the yellow pulp and the white inner peel. Carefully cut one of the two halves in two. Imagine lifting this lemon wedge to your mouth and smelling it. Now bite into the sour, juicy lemon.

Is your mouth watering? If you're like most people, it is.

You have just experienced guided imagery. Guided imagery uses the power of the mind to cause physical changes in the body. You see,

hear, feel, and taste things in your imagination, and your body reacts. (It is called "guided" imagery because usually someone else tells you what to imagine.) Champion athletes have been using guided imagery for years. Before they compete, they repeatedly visualize themselves performing calmly and perfectly. The benefits of guided imagery are so accepted in the world of sports that three out of four Olympic athletes now practice some form of guided imagery.

More recently, doctors have begun using guided imagery with their patients, sometimes with astounding results. Doctors at the Cleveland Clinic in the United States wanted to test the effects of guided imagery on patients who were going to have surgery. So, they did an experiment. They divided 130 patients into two groups. One group (called the "control group") had no special preparation for the surgery. The other group listened to guided imagery tapes for three days before and six days after surgery. With a background of soothing music, the tapes instructed patients to imagine that they were in calm, beautiful surroundings with someone they loved beside them. Then they were encouraged to imagine themselves in the operating room, having the surgery with little pain or fear.

On the day of the surgery, all patients were asked to rate their anxiety level on a scale from 0 to 100, with 0 meaning no anxiety and 100 meaning extreme anxiety. The control group rated their anxiety as 73; the guided imagery group rated their anxiety as 38. Five days after surgery, the difference between the two groups was even more dramatic. The control group rated their anxiety as 55, whereas the guided imagery group rated their anxiety as 10. The guided imagery group not only felt less anxious, they apparently felt less pain. All patients had medication pumps that allowed them to give themselves painkillers as they needed them. The guided imagery group used 37 percent less pain medicine.

The doctors were especially interested in knowing how much pain medicine their patients used because that amount is an objective, measurable quantity. It is a fact that seems to demonstrate the mind's power over the body.

Have you changed your opinion about Sam's using guided imagery to prepare for the test? Why or why not?

PART 2

Experience guided imagery. Read the guided imagery script below. This script is for people who want to relax. After each paragraph, pause and do what the script tells you to do. When you are finished, think about whether you feel more relaxed. If you would like to, share your experience with the class.

Take a deep breath . . . breathing into your belly if you can . . . and breathing all the way out . . .

Feel your breath go to all the tight, tense places in your body . . . and then breathe out all the tension . . .

And now imagine a place where you feel safe and peaceful . . . a place either real or not real . . . a place from your past . . . or somewhere you've always wanted to go . . . it doesn't matter . . . just so it's a place that feels good and safe and peaceful to you . . .

Now look around this place . . . enjoying the colors . . . the scenery . . . seeing each and every detail . . . looking to your left . . . and to your right . . .

Listen to the sounds of the place . . . whatever they might be . . . wind or water or birds . . . enjoying the music of this special place . . .

And feel whatever you're sitting against or lying on . . . or maybe feel the ground beneath your feet . . . whether it's sand or grass or dirt . . . or maybe you're in a comfortable chair . . . or sitting on a nice, warm rock in the sun . . .

Feel the air on your skin . . . maybe cool and dry . . . or warm and wet . . . or maybe you're inside and can feel the warmth of a nice fire on your face and hands . . . or maybe you're outside and can feel a breeze . . .

Smell the air . . . maybe you smell flowers . . . or sea air . . . or sweet grass . . . or pine from the forest . . .

Notice a pleasant energy in the air all around you . . . a feeling that something wonderful is going to happen . . .

Take another deep breath . . . feeling safe and comfortable and relaxed . . .

Whenever you're ready, come back into the room . . . knowing that you can go back to your special place again soon . . .

With a partner, write a guided imagery script for Sam, the young man who panics during tests. If you would like to, read your script in front of the class.

1. PRE-READING

The people in the picture live in the small town of Wetumka, Oklahoma. They are celebrating a festival called "Sucker Day."

The dictionary defines *sucker* as "a foolish person who is easily cheated." It is not a polite word. Here is an example of something a sucker might do:

A man is selling watches on a busy street in New York City. He is selling them for only twenty dollars each. He says they are gold watches, made by a famous company. When people stop to look, he shows them the company's name on the watch. Someone who believes the man and buys a watch is probably a *sucker*.

Look at the picture and think about these questions. Discuss your answers with your classmates.

▸ In your native language, do you have a word similar to the word *sucker*—a word that means "a foolish person who is easily cheated"? What is the word? Tell the class.

▸ Think about the meaning of the word *sucker*. Then look at the picture and read the title of the story on the next page. What could this story possibly be about? Take a guess, and remember that any logical guess is correct.

Sucker Day

In August 1950, a stranger drove into the small town of Wetumka, Oklahoma. He walked into the local newspaper office and introduced himself. He said that his name was F. Morrison and that he was the publicity man for a circus—a big circus, with elephants, tigers, clowns, and acrobats. He had exciting news: The circus was coming to Wetumka! It would arrive in just three weeks, on August 24.

Wetumka was a town of only 2,000 people, and news traveled fast. By late that afternoon, almost everyone in town had heard about the circus. The businesspeople were especially eager to hear more. A circus would bring people to town, and people would spend money in local stores and restaurants. The businesspeople wanted more information about the circus. Did Mr. Morrison have a few minutes to talk to them?

He sure did! He'd be happy to talk to them! He could meet with them at seven o'clock that evening.

At seven o'clock, the businesspeople of Wetumka gathered to hear about the circus. F. Morrison told them that the circus would attract thousands of people, so they'd better get plenty of supplies. And, he added, he wanted to tell them about a special business opportunity.

"Each person who comes to the circus will get a program," he said, "and in those programs, there will be advertisements. I can sell you advertising space right now." The cautious businesspeople of Wetumka looked at F. Morrison and said nothing. "I know, I know. You want to think it over," Mr. Morrison continued. "That's understandable, because advertising space is expensive—in fact, it's very expensive." The businesspeople looked at one another and frowned. "But," he went on, "you'll get more for your money than just advertising space. The circus will buy all its supplies from the businesses that advertise in the program."

"Let me give you an example. A circus sells hot dogs, right? Well, where is the circus going to buy those hot dogs? From the store that advertises in the program! Balloons? Soft drinks? Hay for the elephants? We'll buy them all from the businesses that advertise in the program. And when the circus people get hungry, where will they eat? That's right! At the restaurants that advertise in the program!"

Mr. Morrison told the businesspeople they didn't have to make up their minds right away. He'd be in town for the next two weeks, doing publicity for the circus. They could pay him for advertising space anytime.

During the next two weeks, Mr. Morrison sold advertising space to almost every business in Wetumka. He also became a local hero. He was a friendly man who spent his days walking up and down Main Street, greeting people by name. When it was time for him to leave—he said he had to get back to the circus—people were sorry to see him go. He told everyone he would come back in a week, leading the circus into town. When he left Wetumka, his suitcase was filled with the money that people had paid for advertising space.

On the morning of August 24, crowds of people poured into Wetumka, just as F. Morrison had predicted. By late morning, thousands of people were waiting along Main Street to watch for the circus, which was to arrive at noon.

At noon the circus was nowhere in sight.

At one o'clock, the circus still hadn't come, and the businesspeople realized that they had been tricked. There was no circus! What suckers they were! F. Morrison had cheated them out of their money. But the money was the least of their worries. What were they going to do now about the thousands of people who were waiting for the circus? The crowd was getting more impatient by the minute. What if the hot, tired people became really angry?

The mayor of Wetumka made a quick and wise decision. He told the people that, unfortunately, no circus was coming. Then he immediately declared August 24 "Sucker Day" in Wetumka. He announced that all refreshments were free! The hot dogs, the soft drinks, the ice cream—all free!

This pleased the people so much that they went into local businesses and spent all the

(continued)

money they had brought for the circus. The town businesspeople watched in amazement as their cash registers filled with money.

"Sucker Day" was so successful that the residents of Wetumka decided to celebrate August 24 every year as Sucker Day. There is a parade and free refreshments. It is the biggest event of the year in little Wetumka.

A few years after F. Morrison's visit, the Wetumka police got a phone call from a sheriff in a small town in Missouri. The sheriff said a man named F. Morrison had just been arrested.

Mr. Morrison had sold advertising space in a circus program, but there was no circus. Hadn't he pulled the same trick in Wetumka a few years back? Should the sheriff send Morrison to Oklahoma when he finished his jail sentence in Missouri?

The police chief consulted the businesspeople of Wetumka and then phoned the sheriff in Missouri. No, the people of Wetumka didn't want to bring charges against F. Morrison. Mr. Morrison, they said, was the best thing that had ever happened to Wetumka, Oklahoma.

2. VOCABULARY

◆ **LOOKING AT THE STORY**

Complete the sentences with the words in the box. Write the correct words on the lines.

amazement	attract	eager	greeted	supplies
announced	cautious	frowned	impatient	the least of their worries
arrested	consulted	gathered	sentence	

1. When the businesspeople of Wetumka heard that a circus was coming to town, they were very interested. They were _____*eager*_____ to hear more.

2. At seven o'clock, the businesspeople came together at the town meeting hall. They _____ to listen to Mr. Morrison.

3. The circus would bring a lot of people to Wetumka. Morrison said it would _____ thousands.

4. Morrison said that businesses should buy all the things they needed for crowds of people. "You should get plenty of _____," he said.

5. The businesspeople didn't smile when Morrison said that advertising space was very expensive. They all _____.

6. The businesspeople were very careful with their money. They were _____ people.

7. As Morrison walked up and down Main Street, he said hello to everyone. He _____ everyone by name.

8. The people were tired of waiting for the circus. They were getting more _____ by the minute.

9. The money they had lost was only a small problem for the businesspeople. Actually, it was _____.

10. After he declared August 24 "Sucker Day," the mayor _____ that all refreshments were free.

11. It was a big surprise to the businesspeople of Wetumka that they made money on August 24. They watched in _____ as their cash registers filled.

12. A sheriff in Missouri took Morrison and put him in jail. After the sheriff _____ Morrison, he called the police chief in Wetumka.

13. Morrison's punishment was one year in jail. The sheriff asked, "Should I send him to Oklahoma when he finishes his _____ here?"

14. The police chief asked the businesspeople of Wetumka for their opinion. After he _____ them, he phoned the sheriff in Missouri.

◆ LOOKING AT SPECIAL EXPRESSIONS

Find the best way to complete each sentence. Write the letter of your answer on the line.

***'d better* = should**

_____ 1. Morrison told the businesspeople that the circus would attract thousands of people, so they'd better

_____ 2. I'm going on vacation tomorrow, so I'd better

_____ 3. She has a big test tomorrow, so she'd better

a. stay home and study tonight.

b. pack my suitcase.

c. get plenty of supplies.

***to make up your mind* = to decide**

_____ 4. Morrison told the businesspeople that they could buy advertising space anytime;

_____ 5. The little boy stood at the ice cream stand for five minutes;

_____ 6. She can't decide whether to stay in her apartment or look for a better place;

d. finally, his mother told him he had to make up his mind and choose a flavor.

e. the landlord is giving her until June to make up her mind.

f. they didn't have to make up their minds right away.

3. COMPREHENSION/READING SKILLS

◆ **UNDERSTANDING THE MAIN IDEAS**

Circle the letter of the best answer.

1. Who was F. Morrison?
   a. He was the publicity man for a circus.
   b. He was the editor of the newspaper in Wetumka, Oklahoma.
   c. He was a man who cheated people out of their money.

2. Why were the businesspeople eager to hear about the circus?
   a. A circus would bring people to Wetumka, and people would spend money in local stores and restaurants.
   b. Most of the businesspeople had children who would enjoy the circus.
   c. Wetumka was very small, so there wasn't much to do; a circus would bring some excitement to the town.

3. Why were the businesspeople willing to pay a lot of money for advertising space in the circus program?
   a. Buying advertising space in the circus program was cheaper than other types of advertising.
   b. They thought that a lot of people would see their advertisements.
   c. Morrison told them that the circus would buy its supplies from the businesses that advertised in the program.

4. How successful was F. Morrison at selling advertising space?
   a. Almost every business in Wetumka bought advertising space.
   b. About half the businesses in Wetumka bought advertising space.
   c. The cautious businesspeople in Wetumka didn't buy advertising space, but Morrison was very successful in Missouri.

5. When the circus didn't come, what was the biggest worry of the businesspeople?
   a. They worried most about the money they had lost.
   b. They worried most about selling all the supplies they had bought.
   c. They worried most about the crowd of hot, impatient people.

6. What did the mayor of Wetumka tell the angry crowd?
   a. He promised them that the circus would be there soon.
   b. He announced that all the refreshments were free.
   c. He told them that Morrison had been arrested in Missouri.

7. How do the people of Wetumka celebrate Sucker Day every year?
   a. There is a parade and free refreshments.
   b. There is a free circus.
   c. There is music and dancing.

The underlined information is incorrect. Find the correct information in the story and write it. Work quickly; try to complete this exercise in three minutes or less.

1. In August <u>1952</u>, a stranger drove into the small town of Wetumka, Oklahoma.
   1950

2. He walked into the local <u>real estate</u> office and introduced himself.

3. He said that his name was <u>M</u>. Morrison.

4. Morrison said that a circus would arrive on August <u>23</u>.

5. Morrison said he'd be in town for <u>three</u> weeks, doing publicity for the circus.

6. When Morrison left Wetumka, his <u>briefcase</u> was filled with the money people had paid for advertising space.

7. Thousands of people were waiting along Main Street to watch for the circus, which was to arrive at <u>one o'clock</u>.

8. The <u>police chief</u> of Wetumka declared August 24 Sucker Day.

9. Several years after F. Morrison's visit, the Wetumka police got a call from a sheriff in <u>Kansas</u>.

10. The police chief consulted the businesspeople of Wetumka and then <u>wrote</u> the sheriff that they didn't want to bring charges against Morrison.

4. DISCUSSION

A. Interview a classmate who has information about an unusual festival. Ask your classmate the questions below. Listen carefully and take notes when your classmate answers.

▶ What is the name of the festival?

▶ Where is it?

▶ When is it?

▶ How many people go to the festival?

▶ What happens at the festival?

▶ Do people wear special clothes?

▶ Do people eat special foods?

▶ Do people play games?

▶ Is there music?

▶ Do you know the history of the festival?

▶ Have you ever gone to the festival?

B. This poster advertises Sucker Day in Wetumka.

Make a poster for a festival that you have attended. Draw a picture on your poster and be sure to include:

▶ the name of the festival

▶ the place

▶ the date (You can make up a date.)

▶ the events and the time of each event

Display your poster in the classroom. Answer your classmates' questions about the festival.

5. WRITING

A. Using the information your classmate gave you in the discussion exercise, write a paragraph about an unusual festival. Or write about an unusual festival that you have attended. Here is what one student wrote.

The first weekend in July our little village in Lichtenhorst, Germany, follows a very old tradition and celebrates its annual "Schützenfest." It is in honor of the people in our village who are the best at shooting a rifle.

The most important person of the Schützenfest is the champion shooter (Schützenkönig). He is crowned a few days before the Schützenfest. All male members of the shooting club shoot at a target and try to get a score of 10 three times. The man who gets a score of 30 is crowned Schützenkönig.

Late on Friday afternoon, almost everyone in our village meets at the village hall to march together to the champion shooter's home. He receives a medal and delivers a little speech before inviting all his guests to have drinks, ice cream, and candy with him and his family.

Afterwards everyone marches back to the village hall and the fun part begins. Everyone celebrates by having a big dinner together. A band plays and the waiters are busy carrying huge plates of food to each table. As soon as the dinner is over, people start to dance, and the party goes on until late into the night.

When the music stops, people go home looking forward to next year's Schützenfest in Lichtenhorst.

B. Write the true story of someone you know who was cheated out of his or her money. Or write about an experience you thought was going to be bad that turned out well in the end.

CHALLENGE

F. Morrison told the businesspeople of Wetumka that he had a special opportunity for them. His "business opportunity" was a scam (a dishonest trick), and the businesspeople of Wetumka lost a lot of their money.

Following are some other "opportunities." Read the information carefully. Can you guess which of these opportunities are scams? (Look in the Answer Key to find out which are scams.)

EARN UP TO $2,000 A WEEK IN YOUR OWN HOME CHOOSE YOUR OWN HOURS

We are a Mail Order Company, and we need help stuffing our sales brochures into envelopes. Right now, we have so much work on hand that we are paying home workers $2 for each envelope stuffed and returned to us according to our instructions. There is no limit to the number of envelopes that you can stuff for us. Stuff 250 envelopes and get paid $500 . . . Stuff 500 envelopes and get paid $1,000 . . . Stuff 1,000 envelopes and get paid $2,000.

All envelopes will be sent to you with the addresses already typed on and the postage stamps already affixed. That means that you will not have to address any envelopes or buy any postage stamps. Just stuff the envelopes with our brochures and mail them back to us. As soon as we receive your shipment of stuffed envelopes, we'll rush your paycheck to you along with another set of free supplies for stuffing more envelopes.

As a show of good faith, to show us that you are serious about stuffing envelopes for our company, we're going to request that you send us a REFUNDABLE DEPOSIT of $37. The fee will be returned to you as soon as you send us your first 250 stuffed envelopes. At that time we'll send you a check for $537, to cover payment for 250 stuffed envelopes plus a refund of your $37 deposit.

As soon as we have enough home workers, we will withdraw this offer. So please take action today!

MODELS

Earn $100 per hour or $500 per day as a fashion or commercial model. Full or part time. No experience necessary. Real-people types, such as children, grandmothers, college students, and construction workers welcome. No fee.

Call now to schedule an interview. If you are selected, we will ask you to provide professional photographs. We will distribute your photos to businesses that are looking for "real-people" models—people like YOU!

$2,000 SCHOLARSHIP GUARANTEED

Every year, millions of dollars in scholarships go unclaimed. You can use this money to finance your college education. Simply pay us a $200 scholarship fee, and we will scan our electronic database and match you with a scholarship. If we can't find at least a $2,000 scholarship for you, we will return your $200.

FINAL NOTIFICATION
*****
BRAND-NEW CAR

This is our final notification regarding a brand-new car we will deliver directly to you. The car is being held in a secured facility awaiting your response. Failure to respond by the posted deadline date will result in forfeiture of the car. First, choose the car you would like:

_____ Ford Mustang   _____ Honda Accord

_____ Pontiac Solstice   _____ Toyota Camry

_____ Mitsubishi Eclipse   _____ Dodge Charger

Then mail your check for $21.99 to cover the cost of delivery of your car. This is a nationwide offer to promote the sale of new 1:39-scale model cars. Mail your check for $21.99 today to guarantee delivery of the car of your choice.

$100,000 IN 60 DAYS!

Don't throw this letter away until you have carefully considered what I am about to show you. This could be the most important communication you will ever receive.

FOLLOW THE INSTRUCTIONS BELOW AND IN 20 TO 60 DAYS, YOU WILL RECEIVE $100,000 CASH BY MAIL.

1. Immediately send $5 cash to each of the five names below:

   ▸ Fred Hayward, 451 N. Fourth St., Indiana, PA 15701

   ▸ Jack Gagamov, 13760 Rose Lane, South Holland, IL 60473

   ▸ Jorge Martinez, 7933 Pond Road, Whitewater, WI 53190

   ▸ Alice Quigley, 1354 Norkenzie Ave., Eugene, OR 97401

   ▸ John Harvey, 230 Fresno Ave., Santa Cruz, CA 95060

2. Remove the FIRST name, move the other names up, and place your name in the fifth position.

3. Print 100 copies of this letter showing your name in the fifth position. Mail the 100 letters. (Do not put your return address on the envelopes.)

That's all there is to it! Within 20 to 60 days, you will receive $100,000 in cash. The fact that you have received this letter shows that it works!

1. PRE-READING

The woman in the picture is running through the streets of her city, Sarajevo, in 1992.

Look at the picture and think about these questions. Discuss your answers with your classmates.

▶ In what country is Sarajevo?

▶ Why do you think the woman is running?

▶ Look at the building behind the woman. What do you think happened to the building? Take a guess, and remember that any logical guess is correct.

Love Under Siege

On a Sunday afternoon in the summer of 1992, Eric Adam sat folding laundry in his apartment in Phoenix, Arizona. He was half listening to the news on TV and trying not to think back.

Two years ago, Eric had been happy; he was engaged to marry a wonderful woman named Suzi. But Eric's happiness ended suddenly. Suzi, who had a weak heart, died of a heart attack. She was 33 years old. Now, two years after Suzi's death, Eric was still struggling with his grief. As he sat on his sofa, folding laundry, his thoughts kept returning to Suzi.

The news on TV was about the summer Olympics. A reporter was talking about a young woman from Bosnia. She was a runner who was training for the Olympics. Twice a day, she ran through the streets of Sarajevo. "Sarajevo?" Eric wondered. There was a civil war going on in the city of Sarajevo. How could anyone train for the Olympics in Sarajevo? Eric stopped folding laundry and looked at the TV. On the screen, a young woman in a track suit was running through Sarajevo's streets. She was running with her head held high, even though snipers occasionally tried to shoot her. She ran straight toward the camera and then she was gone. The news report was over.

Eric stared at the TV screen. He was stunned. What courage the woman had! Eric wanted to meet this woman; he wanted to talk to her. That wouldn't be easy. She lived halfway around the world, and Eric didn't even know her name.

Eric went to the library and began looking through newspapers. Finally, he found what he was looking for—a photo of the young woman running through the streets of Sarajevo. Under the photo was the woman's name: Mirsada Buric. From the newspapers, Eric learned that Mirsada was no longer in Sarajevo. She was at the Summer Olympic Games in Barcelona, Spain.

Eric wrote Mirsada a letter. He wrote that he had seen her on TV and wanted her to know that "there is someone in America who admires you." He ended his letter, "If I can help you in any way, please let me know."

Mirsada's Olympic race was the 3,000 meters. Mirsada didn't win, but when she crossed the finish line, the people in the stadium stood and cheered. They had seen Mirsada on TV, running through the streets of Sarajevo. In the eyes of the crowd, Mirsada was a winner.

After the Olympics, Mirsada couldn't return to Sarajevo because it was too dangerous. She went to Slovenia, a country north of Bosnia, as a refugee. Separated from her family, Mirsada was lonely. She thought about Eric's letter and decided to answer it, with the help of her Bosnian-English dictionary. Eric answered her letter and sent a picture of himself. For the next few months, letters flew back and forth between Eric and Mirsada. Finally, Eric wrote Mirsada that he was going to be in Europe on business. He wanted to stop in Slovenia so that he could meet her.

At nine o'clock in the evening, Mirsada stood on a street corner in Slovenia, waiting for Eric. A small car pulled up, and a young man with brown hair and blue eyes stepped out of the car. It was Eric. He ran to Mirsada, smiling. "How are you?" Eric asked. "Fine," Mirsada answered. Then they looked at each other and laughed. Eric couldn't speak Bosnian, and Mirsada couldn't speak English. Eric went to the car and got the woman who was translating for him.

Mirsada, Eric, and the translator went to Mirsada's small apartment, where Eric and Mirsada began to talk. They talked until sunrise. Then Eric had to go. If he didn't leave within the hour, he would miss his flight back to the United States. As he walked toward the car, Eric saw the sadness in Mirsada's eyes. Suddenly he said, "Do you want to come to the United States? There'd be no strings attached—I'll buy a round-trip ticket, so you can go home anytime." Mirsada began to cry. "No," she answered. "Thank you. But no." Eric kissed Mirsada on the cheek and said, "Well, if you ever change your mind, the offer stands." Then he was gone.

Mirsada thought about Eric's offer for weeks. Finally, she decided to go to the United States.

In March 1993, nine months after Eric first saw her on TV, Mirsada arrived in Phoenix, Arizona. She moved into Eric's apartment,

(continued)

where she and Eric lived together like a brother and a sister. Mirsada studied English. She started college classes. She ran in dozens of races and won most of them. And, she fell in love with Eric, who was already in love with her. In December, they were married.

In the summer of 1996, the Olympic torch passed through Phoenix, Arizona, on its way to the Games in Atlanta, Georgia. Mirsada was chosen to carry the torch through Phoenix. As Mirsada ran through the cheering crowd, she thought about everything she had done since the last Olympics. She had come to the United States, learned English, and graduated from college. She had won races. She had fallen in love and gotten married. And now she was carrying the Olympic torch through the streets of Phoenix. She ran as she had run through the streets of Sarajevo—with her head held high.

2. VOCABULARY

◆ LOOKING AT THE STORY

Complete the sentences with the words in the box. Write the correct words on the lines.

admires	grief	occasionally	thoughts kept returning
cheered	laundry	refugee	track suit
engaged	no strings attached	stunned	trained

1. Eric washed his clothes. Then he sat on the sofa and folded his
   _____*laundry*_____.

2. Eric was going to get married. He was _____ to a woman named Suzi.

3. Eric was fighting his feelings of sadness about Suzi's death. He was still struggling with his _____.

4. Eric couldn't stop thinking about Suzi. His _____ to her.

5. The runner on TV was preparing for the Olympics. She _____ by running through the streets of Sarajevo twice a day.

6. In the picture on page 130, Mirsada is wearing a _____.

7. Sometimes, men with guns tried to kill people in Sarajevo. Mirsada ran even though snipers _____ tried to shoot her.

8. Eric was very surprised to see a woman running through the streets of Sarajevo; he couldn't believe it. When the news report was over, he stared at the TV screen and didn't move. He was _____.

9. After seeing her on TV, Eric had a high opinion of Mirsada. He wrote her, "Someone in the United States _____ you."

10. When Mirsada crossed the finish line, the people in the stadium shouted with happiness. They _____ because they knew Mirsada; they had seen her on TV, running through the streets of Sarajevo.

11. Mirsada couldn't return to her country because it was too dangerous. So, she went to Slovenia as a _____.

12. Eric told Mirsada he would buy her a round-trip ticket to the United States. He didn't want anything from her in return. He told her that there would be

_____.

♦ **LOOKING AT A NEW CONTEXT**

Complete the sentences to show that you understand the meanings of the new words. Then in small groups, take turns reading your sentences aloud. When your classmates read their answers, follow up with comments and questions, such as "Really?" "Why?" or "Me too."

1. Something I do only occasionally is _____.

2. Someone whose courage I admire is _____.

3. A sports team I cheer for is _____.

4. An Olympic sport I would love to train for is _____.

5. A person my thoughts keep returning to is _____.

6. A place my thoughts keep returning to is _____.

3. COMPREHENSION/READING SKILLS

♦ **UNDERSTANDING CAUSE AND EFFECT**

Find the best way to complete each sentence. Write the letter of your answer on the line.

_____ 1. Eric was struggling with grief

_____ 2. Eric couldn't believe a runner was training in Sarajevo

_____ 3. Eric wanted to meet Mirsada

_____ 4. For a week, Eric looked through newspapers

_____ 5. As she ran through the streets of Phoenix, Mirsada held her head high

a. because he wanted to know the name of the Bosnian runner he had seen on TV.

b. because there was a war there.

c. because she was proud of everything she had done.

d. because Suzi had died.

e. because he admired her courage.

◆ UNDERSTANDING SUPPORTING DETAILS

Read each sentence on the left. Which sentence on the right gives you more information? Match the sentences. Write the letter of your answer on the line.

_____ 1. Eric was happy.

_____ 2. The reporter on TV was talking about a young woman from Bosnia.

_____ 3. Eric sent Mirsada a letter.

_____ 4. Mirsada's race was the 3,000 meters.

_____ 5. Mirsada thought about everything she had done.

a. She was a runner who was training for the Olympics by running through the streets of Sarajevo twice a day.

b. He was engaged to marry a wonderful woman named Suzi.

c. He wrote that he had seen Mirsada on TV and that he admired her.

d. She had come to the United States, learned English, graduated from college, won races, fallen in love, and gotten married.

e. She didn't win, but people cheered when she crossed the finish line.

4. DISCUSSION

A. Eric and Mirsada had a baby in 1998. When their daughter is older, they can tell her the amazing story of how they met.

What about your parents? Your grandparents? Your married classmates? How did they meet? Interview someone who is married. First, with the help of your classmates and your teacher, make a list of questions you could ask, such as:

▶ How old were you when you met?

▶ Where did you meet?

▶ What did you think when you saw her/him for the first time?

▶ _____

▶ _____

▶ _____

Ask someone who is married the questions. Listen carefully and write down the answers. Then tell the class what you learned.

B. The story "Love Under Siege" ends in 1996, with Mirsada carrying the Olympic torch through the streets of Phoenix. What do you think Mirsada is doing now? Does she still run in races? What does she do for a living? Where does she live? Is she still married to Eric? Take a guess, and remember that any logical guess is correct.

In a small group, tell your guesses to a secretary. The secretary will write down the group's guesses and read them to the class. Then read the true story of Mirsada's life from 1996 to the present in the Answer Key.

5. WRITING

Write the love story of how you or someone you know met his/her spouse. Here is what one student wrote.

When I was 24 years old, I came to the United States from Mexico to live with my aunt. I was her housekeeper. My aunt and her sons treated me very badly. My day started at 5:00 A.M. I had to cook all their meals, clean their shoes, and pick up their clothes. I had to clean the house very well because when my aunt came home, she wiped her hand over the furniture looking for dust. When everybody went to sleep, I began to iron.

In the spring, I did the ironing on an enclosed porch with lots of windows. Every night, a young man stood on the porch next door and watched me iron, but he never spoke to me.

One summer day, I went to the store, and he started walking by my side. For the first time, he spoke to me. He wondered why they treated me so badly. His house was so close that he could hear when they screamed at me. He told me if I wanted to go back to Mexico, he would buy me an airplane ticket, but I did not go. I needed the $10 a week that my aunt paid me and that I sent to my family in Mexico.

That was 29 years ago. I am married to the man who was looking at me on the porch. We celebrated our 28th anniversary. I love him very much. He is a caring man with a big heart, and he is a wonderful father and husband. I thank God for him.

Mirsada Buric did not win the 3,000-meter race at the Olympics—she finished thirty-first out of thirty-three runners—yet her race is considered one of the great moments in Olympic history. Following are some other great Olympic stories. The ending of each story is missing. What is the rest of the story?

Read each story and look at the photo that goes with it. If you know the ending of the story, write it. If you don't know the ending of the story, take a guess and write a possible ending.

◆1 Kip Keino, Kenya, Track and Field

On the morning of his 1,500-meter race at the 1968 Games, runner Kip Keino of Kenya was riding in a taxi to the Olympic Stadium in Mexico City. He was worried. There were traffic jams all over the city, and his taxi was barely moving. Keino kept looking ahead at the cars, buses, and taxis in front of him, and then down at his watch. It was an hour before his race, then fifty minutes, then forty minutes, then thirty minutes. Finally, it was only twenty minutes before the start of the race. And the taxi was still 2 kilometers from the stadium.

For the past several days, Keino had been suffering from severe stomach pains, and doctors thought he probably had an infection. Earlier that morning, he had been worried that he might not run well. Now he was worried that he might not run at all. At the rate the taxi was traveling, he couldn't possibly get to the race on time.

Did Keino get to the race on time? If so, how did he do it?

_____

_____

_____

_____

_____

_____

◆2 Vera Caslavska, Czechoslovakia (now the Czech Republic), Gymnastics

Gymnast Vera Caslavska had won three gold medals and one silver medal at the 1964 Games in Tokyo, and she was the favorite to win again at the Games in Mexico City in 1968. But just a few months before the Games, politics almost prevented her from competing in the Olympics at all.

In 1968, Czechoslovakia (now the Czech Republic) was still controlled by the Soviet Union. Many people in Czechoslovakia, including Caslavska, wanted to be free of that control. In April 1968, she signed a document called the "Manifesto of 2,000 Words," which demanded Czechoslovakia's independence from the Soviet Union. A short time later, Soviet tanks rolled into Prague. Caslavska's friends warned her that she was in danger of being arrested, so she went to a small village in the mountains. It was just two months before the Olympics, and Caslavska needed to practice. But there was no gym in the village and none of the equipment a gymnast needed.

How did Caslavska train for the Olympics? Did she go to the Games in Mexico City? If so, what happened there?

_____

_____

_____

_____

_____

_____

_____

_____

3 Derek Redmond, Great Britain, Track and Field

Derek Redmond was a great runner who had a lot of injuries. By the time of the 1992 Olympics in Barcelona, he had already had five operations. The latest operation, on his foot, was just four months before the Games began. But he recovered well from the surgery, and in Barcelona, everything seemed to be going his way. He had an excellent chance of winning the gold medal in the 400-meter race.

Redmond easily won the quarterfinal race. Next came the semifinal. Redmond was in the lead as the runners went around the first bend in the track. Suddenly, he felt a sharp pain in the back of his leg and dropped to the ground in agony. A muscle had torn. When he looked up and saw paramedics coming toward him with a stretcher, he made up his mind: They would not carry him off the track. He immediately jumped up and began limping toward the finish line.

Did Redmond finish the semifinal race? If so, how did he do it?

_____

_____

_____

_____

_____

_____

Check the Answer Key to find out the true ending of each story.

To the Teacher

All Units

Pre-Reading

If your students need extra support, you might want to tell them the story before they read it, stopping well short of the ending. As you tell the story, draw pictures on the board to illustrate it. Following are some tips for drawing.

1. Keep it simple! To draw a person, just drawing the head and shoulders suffices most of the time—no need to draw arms, legs, feet, ears. A few squiggles to represent hair indicates the person is female; no squiggles indicates a male. Smaller heads and shoulders are children. Add two dots for the eyes, a dot for the nose, and a line for the mouth, and the figure is complete.

2. Use the same symbols consistently to represent the same things so that students get used to your drawing style. For example, two parallel lines with a triangle-shaped roof (resembling a child's drawing of a house) represent a building. A dollar sign inside means the building is a bank; a shopping cart indicates it is a supermarket.

3. Draw nouns to represent verbs. For example, draw a knife to represent *to cut*.

4. Feel free to move back and forth between drawing images from the story and acting out scenes. You can even pretend to pick up items you drew on the board (such as a teacup) and use them as props in your reenactment of a scene.

Drawing tips 1–3 are the suggestions of Norma Shapiro, whose reference book

Chalk Talks (Command Performance Language Institute, 1994) has further tips and hundreds of examples of simple drawings.

Vocabulary

It is important to encourage students to devise a system for learning new words at home—keeping a vocabulary notebook, for example, or writing the words on flashcards and storing them in envelopes labeled *Know* and *Don't know*. Students might also want to try the "four corners" technique of reviewing vocabulary. The steps are as follows:

1. Fold a piece of notebook-sized paper in half. Then fold it in half again. Cut or tear the paper along the folds so that you have four small pieces of paper.

2. Fold each small piece of paper in half. Then fold it in half again so that the paper is divided into four sections.

3. In the upper left section, write the target word.

4. In the upper right section, draw a picture that will help you remember the word (if you can).

5. In the lower left section, write a sentence containing the word, but do not write the word. Leave a blank space where the word would go.

6. In the lower right section, write the translation of the word in your native language or copy the definition of the word from an English-language dictionary.

7. To review the word, fold the paper so that you can see any section but the one in which the word is written. Try to recall the target word.

Unit 1 Love at First Sight

Teaching Tips

Story: The story introduces the modal auxiliary *might* and the conditional with *would* (used here in its negative form, *wouldn't*). It is not necessary to go into long explanations. You can simply explain that *might* comes in front of another verb and means "maybe." *Wouldn't* also comes in front of another verb and means "probably not." A lesson for another day might be the three uses of *would*:

▸ past of *will* (*He said he would come.*)

▸ to make a polite request (*Would you please open the door?*)

▸ in conditional sentences to show what is likely (*If I had enough money, I would buy a new car.*)

Discussion: All of the statements are true. (One might say "unfortunately true.") If students question the veracity of a statement, you might want to tell them about the research that supports it. The research is summarized below.

1. *In political elections, the more handsome man usually wins.*

   Researchers showed college students photos of pairs of men who had run for political office. The researchers asked the students to guess which man had won, based just on looks. In other words, the students were told to "vote" for the more handsome man. They chose the man who had actually won 69 percent of the time.

2. *In presidential elections, the taller man usually wins.*

   Beginning in 1952, television made it possible for voters to see which candidate was taller when the candidates stood side by side. In the fourteen elections since then, the taller man has been elected president ten times; the shorter man has been elected four times. Only Richard Nixon (in 1972), Jimmy Carter (in 1976),

and George W. Bush (in 2000 and 2004) were shorter than their opponents. (And every U.S. president since 1896 has been taller than the average man in the United States.)

3. *Tall people make more money than short people.*

   One study determined that each inch of height adds $789 a year to a person's yearly salary. So a man who is six feet tall earns, on average, $2,367 more than a man who is five feet, nine inches.

4. *Teachers think attractive students are smarter than unattractive students.*

   Researchers gave fictional academic records to fifth-grade teachers. Each record contained a bogus report card (with above-average grades). Attached to the file was a photo of either an attractive or unattractive student. Teachers were asked to look over each academic record and then estimate the IQ of the student. Teachers estimated the IQs of attractive students to be higher than those of unattractive students.

5. *Attractive people make more money than unattractive people.*

   Two economists, Dr. Daniel Hamermesh at the University of Texas and Dr. Jeff Biddle at Michigan State University, studied the relationship between attractiveness and salary. In a 1993 paper titled "Beauty and the Labor Market," they wrote, "Plain people earn less than people of average looks, who earn less than the good-looking." They discovered that attractive people earn about 12 percent more than unattractive people.

6. *People usually marry people who are about as attractive as they are.*

   There are many studies that show this is true. One of the best-known studies was done in 1972 by Dr. Bernard Murstein. He photographed engaged couples, first together and then separately. He mixed up the individual photos and then gave them to judges. He asked the judges to look at each picture and rate the person's attractiveness on a scale of 1 to 5. When Dr. Murstein paired the photos up, matching the women with their fiancés, he discovered that the judges had given the man and woman in each pair about the same rating. For example, a woman whose attractiveness was rated 3 was usually engaged to a man whose attractiveness was also rated 3.

7. *Babies look at the faces of attractive people longer than they look at the faces of unattractive people.*

In the late 1980s, Judith Langlois at the University of Texas put three- and six-month-old babies in front of a screen and then showed them pairs of photos. One photo in each pair was of a face that was judged by adults to be attractive; the other photo was of a face judged to be unattractive. The infants gazed significantly longer at the attractive face.

8. *Attractive people who have a problem get more help than unattractive people.*

Scientific research shows that people go out of their way to help attractive people. NBC News tested that finding in an unscientific experiment. They put two men and two women on the streets of New York City. One man and one woman were attractive models. The other man and woman were average-looking. All four people were the same race, about the same age, and well-dressed. Each person dropped a folder of papers on the sidewalk while a hidden camera recorded what happened. People stopped to help the two attractive people pick up the papers but did not stop to help the average-looking people.

Next, the four people took turns standing on a street corner and looking lost. People stopped to ask the two attractive people if they needed directions but did not stop to help the two average-looking people.

Unit 2   The Semong (The Tsunami)

The focus of this unit is on a story, passed from generation to generation, that saved thousands of lives on the island closest to the epicenter of the 2004 earthquake in the Indian Ocean. However, if you have students who were directly affected by the 2004 tsunami, you may wish to skip this unit. You can simply say that you think it is a little too soon to read about it.

In the pre-reading section, students are asked to contribute what they know about the 2004 tsunami. News sources reported conflicting figures, so it is quite possible that students will provide differing pieces of information. For example, estimates of the magnitude of the earthquake that caused the tsunami range from 9.0 to 9.3; estimates of the death toll range from 150,000 in early reports to 283,100 in more recent reports; and the number of countries affected by the tsunami varies, depending on how one defines "affected." The following facts are from the Web sites of the United States Geological Survey and National Geographic.

▸ Magnitude of the earthquake: 9.0

▸ Date: Sunday, December 26, 2004

▸ Time: 7:58:53 A.M. local time

▸ Location: in the Indian Ocean, off the western coast of northern Sumatra, Indonesia, just north of Simeulue island

▸ Duration of the earthquake: approximately 10 minutes

▸ Place in history: the fourth-largest earthquake in the world since 1900 and the largest since the 1964 Prince William Sound, Alaska, earthquake

▸ Death toll: more than 283,100 dead; 14,100 still listed as missing

▸ Number of people displaced: 1,126,900

- Animal deaths: very few (Animals fled for higher ground minutes before the tsunami, so they must have sensed it coming.)

- Number of countries reporting severe damage and casualties: 10 (Sumatra, Indonesia, India, Bangladesh, Malaysia, Maldives, Myanmar, Singapore, Sri Lanka, and Thailand)

- Maximum height of tsunami waves: 30 meters (100 feet)

- Distance the tsunami traveled: nearly 5,000 kilometers (3,000 miles) to Africa, where it arrived with enough force to kill people and destroy property. It caused minor damage at two places on the west coast of Australia, and water level fluctuations occurred in wells in various parts of the United States.

- Cause: The earthquake was caused by the release of stresses that had accumulated for centuries at the boundaries of two of the earth's tectonic plates: the India and the Burma plates.

Teaching Tip

Discussion: The exercise works best when many parts of the world are represented in class. If only one country or only two or three countries are represented, you might want to substitute one of the activities below for the one in the text. The first activity works well when the students are from at least two countries; the second is suited for classes in which all the students are from the same country.

1. Students draw roughly sketched maps of their countries on their own paper, marking with an X the places where natural disasters have occurred. Then, using the map as a focal point, they tell a partner from a different country about the natural disasters, sharing personal experiences if they wish to

do so. Model the activity first by drawing a map of your country on the board.

2. While you are out of the room, a student volunteer draws a map of the students' country on the board. The volunteer marks with an X the places where natural disasters have occurred while the class makes suggestions. When you come back into the room, ask the class about the places marked with an X, inviting students to share personal experiences if they wish to do so. Before leaving the room, model the activity by drawing a map of your country on the board.

Unit 3 More Alike Than Different

Friendship Force International was organized in Atlanta, Georgia, in 1977. It is now active in more than 60 countries, including Vietnam and Iran. Friendship Force International was nominated for the Nobel Peace Prize in 1992.

Teaching Tips

Discussion: To turn Exercise B into a whole-class activity, draw the graph on the board, replacing the numbers 1, 2, and 3 with, respectively, a (very) happy face, a sad face, and a neutral face (with a faint smile). Students come to the board and put an X on the line at the place that reflects the way they feel. More often than not, students will put their X in a predictable place; that is, those who have lived in a new country from six weeks to six months will put their X on the descending line, while students who have been in the new country longer will put their X on the ascending line. This activity reassures students that their feelings reflect normal stages in cultural acclimation and are shared by others in the class. Point out that the ascending line to the "at home" stage is more gradual than the steeper and shorter descending line to the sad state, and remind students that it generally takes a year or two to reach that final stage.

Following are two additional discussion activities that go well with this unit.

1. If you would like to emphasize the "more alike than different" theme of the story, you might want to try the following variation on the "Find Someone Who" activity. It is suggested by Peter Grundy in his resource book *Beginners* (Oxford University Press, 1994). In this version, students try to find classmates who are similar to them in some ways. First, students fill in the left side of the chart. Then they move around the classroom, trying to fill in the right side of the chart with names of classmates. Here, for example, are some possible sentences for the chart:

a. I really like _____ and so does _____.

b. I feel happy when _____ and so does _____.

c. I get angry when _____ and so does _____.

d. I like to spend the evening _____ and so does _____.

e. I'm good at _____ and so is _____.

f. I'm not good at _____ and neither is _____.

g. I think the best way to learn English is _____ and so does _____.

In the course of completing the activity, many students discover they have a lot in common with classmates who, on the surface, seem quite unlike them.

2. If you would like to talk about cross-cultural issues, you might want to try the activity below, which teacher-trainer Dorothy Brown contributed to the resource book *New Ways in Teaching Adults* (TESOL, 1997). At the top of the chart, students write in the name of the country where they are living now. They fill in the chart and then, in small groups, compare answers. If all the students are in the same situation (i.e., they are all high school or university students, or they are all in the workforce), you could narrow the discussion by making the heading a specific environment, such as "at work," "at school," or "at the university."

Which things in _____
(*present country*)

impress you?

confuse you?

surprise you?

annoy you?

worry you?

This activity, like the preceding one, can be a social unifier; often students who are superficially different discover they are impressed, confused, surprised, etc., by the same things.

Unit 4 Healthy Again

In the last few decades, acupuncture has become more widely practiced in the West. In 1992, for example, the number of licensed acupuncturists in the United States was 5,500. By 2006, that number had grown to 23,000. Still, acupuncture remains a controversial treatment in some Western medical circles. Skeptics point out that approximately twenty-five percent of all injuries and illnesses resolve on their own and that the placebo effect is powerful, so studies that report patients' subjective improvements in their pain or illness are inconclusive. They call for scientifically controlled studies in which one group of patients receives acupuncture and another group receives a placebo. Researchers in Great Britain are designing studies that would give one group true acupuncture and another group sham acupuncture (pricking with needles, but no insertion of needles). The skeptics say they will believe that acupuncture works only when studies like these indicate that it does. The growing popularity of acupuncture, however, attests to the fact that many patients have already made up their minds.

Unit 5 If You Have Time

The story states that Mr. Garibian immigrated to the United States via Syria but does not state his country of origin. It is actually Iraq, although he is ethnically Armenian. His family was driven from Armenia during the Genocide of 1915 and ended up in Iraq. During a time of social and religious unrest in Iraq, Mr. Garibian was forced to flee to Syria, where he stayed with the cousin in the story. From Syria, he made his way to the United States. Natalie's mother is also ethnically Armenian but grew up in Marseilles, France.

It turned out that two of the cousin's daughters had indeed settled in Paris. Their mother happened to be visiting them at the time Natalie went to the Armenian church. It was pure coincidence that she and Natalie attended the same service.

The story first appeared in *The Palm Beach Post*. When the paper invited readers to share their experiences with angels, Natalie Garibian responded with a first-person essay about finding a relative in a church in Paris. She ended her essay: "I was going to Paris to collect stories to fill my journal and my memories. I was going to Paris to find myself. And that is the beauty of it all. I never looked at those pictures, and I never intended on finding anyone. I didn't have to. My angel found me."

Natalie, a graduate of Duke University, has had her work produced and published nationally. She recently wrote the biography of film producer Howard Minsky, chronicling his incredible six decades in movies, and is developing this Paris story for television.

Teaching Tip

Discussion: In addition to the topics presented in the exercises, the topic of homesickness is appropriate for this unit. To keep the discussion upbeat, ask students to make a list of memories from their countries that cheer them up and then share their lists with the class. For example:

▸ my brother laughing

▸ the sound of traffic in my city

▸ the aromas coming from my mother's kitchen

Unit 6 The Buried City

Some students may wonder if there is any danger of Vesuvius erupting again. Indeed there is. It is one of the world's most dangerous volcanoes, and some 3.5 million Italians live near it. Monitoring devices are in place to warn of activity within the mountain.

Unit 7 Misunderstandings

When the bus driver pulled over, some passengers thought it had something to do with the "bum" in the bathroom, while others thought it had something to do with a bomb. They all poured off the bus, including the man who had been hiding in the restroom. After questioning passengers for forty-five minutes, police began to suspect there had been some sort of misunderstanding but, to be on the safe side, continued to search the bus for another hour. News reports do not say if the man with thirty-five cents in his pocket was allowed to continue his free journey on the bus.

Unit 8 A Real Bargain

Edward Jones's discovery of the map (which he still has not sold) was not by pure luck. He has studied fine art and music for more than twenty years, and when he walks through a thrift store or flea market, he has a pretty good idea of what he is looking for. Just one year after he discovered the map, he bought a musical score from a vendor at a Florida flea market. It turned out to be the original score of an operetta by a Spanish composer—a work that was thought to be lost. It was valued at $850,000.

Unit 9 Black Cats and Broken Mirrors

The men mentioned in the story belonged to the original Friday the 13th Club. Founded in Philadelphia in 1936, the club met every Friday the 13th for one hour. The meetings always ended exactly at 1:13 P.M., which is 13:13 military time. The club had only thirteen members; a newcomer was admitted only if a member died. The club's rules specified that the club's last meeting would be on the last Friday in the 20th century, so the club met on October 13, 2000, and then disbanded. However, other Friday the 13th clubs have sprung up around the country.

According to *Smithsonian Magazine*, U.S. businesses lose an estimated $750 million annually because many people won't shop, travel, or take any unnecessary risks on Friday the 13th.

Unit 10 Flight 5390

The story states that "wind" sucked everything out of the airplane. More precisely, it was sudden decompression caused by the difference in pressure between the air inside and outside the airplane. The force was so strong that it pulled the cockpit door off its hinges and an oxygen tank out of the bolts that held it to the floor. Had the copilot not had both his lap belt and shoulder harness on (the pilot had his lap belt on but had unbuckled his shoulder harness after takeoff), he would no doubt have been pulled out through the pilot's window.

When the pilot was sucked out of the plane, his shirt and undershirt were pulled off his back and his upper body was folded backwards so that he was lying face up on top of the airplane. Some ten minutes later, when Nigel lost his grip, the pilot slipped so that he was bent sideways around the plane, his face banging against the side window.

From his hospital bed, the pilot told reporters from the *Times*, "I was conscious for some of the time. I tried to shout back to the crew, but I'm sure they could not hear me. I think the temperature when I was hanging out the window must have been about minus thirty degrees Celsius. It was extremely fast and frantic. My first recollection of the whole thing was a bang, then I was sucked outside. My first thought after that was that I should keep breathing. Alistair (the copilot) and the crew were magnificent. If it was not for them, I would not be here. It was a miraculous piece of flying."

Both the pilot and copilot returned to flying. Flight attendant Nigel Ogden attempted to return, but he suffered from postraumatic stress and eventually had to find a different line of work.

After reading the Challenge section, some students wondered why the TVs were left on during the emergency aboard JetBlue Flight 292. It is the policy of JetBlue to let the pilot decide whether or not to turn off the TVs. In spite of the incident on Flight 292, a JetBlue spokeswoman announced that JetBlue would not be changing its policy.

Passengers said the information they got from the TV was quite different from the information they got from the pilot. Passenger Pia Varma, 23, said, "The captain apologized, saying there was no problem with the landing gear and that it was no big deal; there was nothing really to worry about. Then, on the news, they're saying this kind of landing has never been attempted before and it's the scariest thing ever. It was a little nerve-racking."

Teaching Tips

Pre-Reading: Because the reading contains many specialized words related to airplanes, students might find it helpful to complete the vocabulary exercise before they read the story.

Discussion: In Exercise B, students take notes in the form of pictures while listening to a classmate's story and then use those pictures as cues when retelling the story in their own words. Intermediate-level learners are certainly able to take written notes, but they might find it worthwhile to practice this technique. Many public-speaking coaches recommend using sketches, rather than the written word, to jog one's memory when speaking before an audience.

Unit 11 A Killer in the Back Seat

Perhaps the most persistent and insidious urban legend in the United States is the "razor blade in the Halloween candy" story. After examining police records, sociologists have determined that virtually all reports of candy tampering were hoaxes. Gerald

Horiuchi, one of the researchers, says, "We are not saying not to inspect treats; you might find something unsanitary. We are not saying just turn the kids loose and let them go." But he does believe there is no truth to the dangerous Halloween candy story.

Unit 12 The Treasure Hunt

When we left this story in the second edition of *Even More True Stories,* investors were trying to raise $10 million for another search. They did not succeed in raising that amount, so ultimately investors sank, both figuratively and literally, $3 million, not $10 million, into exploring the hole.

Speculation regarding who constructed the hole and what lies at its bottom abounds. Many people do not believe the hole and the tunnels that lead to it could have been built by a band of pirates. They maintain that the interconnecting system is so complicated (one expert says its designer had a "devious mind") that only a nation could have devised it. One long-held theory is that the British government built it to hide Incan gold that the British had taken from Spanish ships returning from the New World.

Still others claim the hole and tunnels were not constructed by a band of pirates or a nation, but are, in fact, natural phenomena. They maintain that the hole is nothing more than a sinkhole—a depression in the earth that formed when the ground settled over an empty space in the underlying rock. The oak platforms that searchers found every ten feet could have been fallen trees that sank into the depression, and the tunnels could be naturally occurring caverns. As evidence to support their theory, they point to sinkholes found on the mainland opposite the island. This theory does not explain the artifacts, such as the heart-shaped stone, that purportedly were found in the hole. Neither does it explain the coconut fibers.

The story behind the Beale ciphers seems probable. There is evidence that Morriss (the innkeeper) and Ward (the man who devoted his life to the ciphers) did exist. And Thomas Beale almost certainly did. Using the census of 1790 and other documents, a historian has determined that several Thomas Beales were born in Virginia around that time. Gold and silver certainly could have been discovered in the American West. Why, then, has no one been able to decode the two ciphers, even with the help of computers? Some people think the ciphers may be based on a private, rather than a public, document— perhaps a letter or essay that Beale himself wrote. If that document is lost, the ciphers will never be decoded.

At times, the hills of Bedford Country, Virginia, are crawling with people looking for Beale's treasure. One popular theory among "Bealers," as the searchers are called, is that the treasure is hidden under fake, coded tombstones in one of the forty cemeteries in the area. A Pennsylvania woman spent two months in the Bedford County jail after being caught digging with a backhoe in a cemetery in the middle of the night. The woman found what one would expect to find under tombstones: bodies, not treasure.

Unit 13 The Plain People

The Challenge section presents a problem that the Amish have faced in recent years: The high price of farmland has made it difficult for their growing population to buy land. With the Amish population doubling every twenty years, the problem is escalating. Some Amish have emigrated from the United States to countries like Costa Rica, where land is more affordable. Amish who stay in the United States are frequently choosing to own small businesses rather than farms. Some popular enterprises are roofing companies, construction companies, and fabric stores. Furniture-making is still a popular choice. Ninety percent of those who are born Amish remain in the sect, so unless the birth rate begins to fall, the Amish population will continue to grow exponentially, and the Amish will probably continue to move away from farming.

In the reading, the Amish population is given as 200,000. That figure is an estimate, as the Amish do not participate in the U.S. census. Population figures are generally compiled by examining Amish directories, which contain lists of families.

Unit 14 Does Death Take a Holiday?

Sociologists have also studied death rates among famous people around the time of their birthdays and among Christians around Christmas and Easter. Their findings have been inconclusive. Some studies indicate that people do postpone their deaths until after these events, while other studies do not.

One possible explanation for the differing data is that sociologists are assuming the importance of the events. That could explain, for example, why the earlier study of the death rate among Chinese women around the time of the Harvest Moon Festival showed a dip before the festival while the later study did not. Perhaps the holiday has diminished in importance among Chinese-Americans (although the researcher who studied the death rate from 1985 to 2000 doubts that explanation). Some sociologists contend that future researchers will need to ask subjects how important the event is to them rather than assume its importance.

To the Teacher

Unit 15 Sucker Day

The Wetumka Chamber of Commerce reports that once Sucker Day had been established as an annual—and successful—event, the forgiving townspeople contacted Morrison and asked him to lead the Sucker Day Parade. He said he would if they sent him the money for a bus ticket to Wetumka. Not wanting to risk being fooled again, the townspeople decided to ask someone else to lead the parade.

In material distributed by the Wetumka Chamber of Commerce, its citizens maintain that "Sucker Day in no way honors Morrison, who was a con man. The original celebration was staged to prove that the townspeople could laugh at their mistakes. Today the event means that and much more."

Teaching Tip

Discussion: In the resource book *Gold Mine* (Tango Publications, Montreal, 1993), Melvin Shantz describes an activity that goes nicely with this unit. It is called "Which Story Is True?" Three students sit in chairs facing the class. Each student has a file folder. One folder contains a picture. (He suggests using a frame from a comic strip, but almost any picture will do.) The other two folders contain blank pieces of paper. The student who has the picture describes it; the other two students make up descriptions and try to trick their classmates into believing they are describing something real (in the style of the infamous F. Morrison). The class has to guess which of the three students is describing a real picture and which two are making up descriptions.

This story presents an opportunity to warn students about the scams used in identity theft. They should be cautioned about disclosing credit card, bank account, and social security numbers.

Unit 16 Love Under Siege

Following is information about Sarajevo. It is from the Web site The History Place.

After World War II, the victorious Allies created the multicultural country of Yugoslavia, merging together Slovenia, Croatia, Bosnia, Serbia, Montenegro, and two self-governing provinces, Kosovo and Vojvodina. The new country was composed of ethnic and religious groups that historically had been bitter enemies. Three of these groups were Serbs, who were Orthodox Christian; Croats, who were Catholic; and ethnic Albanians, who were Muslim.

In the years after the war, Tito held the country together, but it plunged into chaos following his death in 1980. Slobodan Milosevic took advantage of the disorder and gained power, using religious hatred as a tool. By the late 1980s, he was Yugoslavia's new leader.

In 1992, the United States and the European Community recognized Bosnia's independence from Yugoslavia. Bosnia was a mostly Muslim country with a thirty-two percent Serb minority. Milosevic, a Serb, responded by attacking Sarajevo, the capital, which was best known internationally for hosting the 1984 Winter Olympics. Serb snipers routinely shot at civilians in Sarajevo. It was during this time that Mirsada Buric ran defiantly through her city's streets. Throughout Bosnia, Muslims were terrorized into leaving their villages, and many were confined to concentration camps. Buric, a Muslim, spent two weeks in one such camp only a few months before the Olympics.

NATO intervention finally ended the conflict in 1995. It is estimated that 200,000 Muslims were systematically murdered while Milosevic was in power.

Answer Key

Unit 1

LOOKING AT THE STORY
1. dizzy
2. unconscious
3. nearby
4. stroke
5. might
6. sight
7. adjust
8. handyman
9. come over
10. clogged
11. owe
12. accepted
13. threw on some clothes

FORMING MENTAL IMAGES AS YOU READ
1. Neighbors found her lying on the ground, unconscious.
2. Pamela was washing dishes and realized that the water wasn't going down the drain in her kitchen sink.
3. He fixed the sink in just a few minutes.
4. Pamela made some tea, and she and Mitch sat at her kitchen table and talked.
5. She turned her head on the pillow and saw the hands on the alarm clock next to her bed.
6. She could see the flowers, the trees, the houses across the street.
7. Mitch thought about Pamela's phone call as he threw on some clothes.
8. He ran the half mile to Pamela's house.
9. "Yes!" Pamela said and threw her arms around Mitch.

UNDERSTANDING CAUSE AND EFFECT
1. c   2. a   3. e   4. b   5. d

DISCUSSION
All of the statements are true.

Unit 2

LOOKING AT THE STORY
1. island
2. village
3. crashed
4. wide
5. paused
6. yelled
7. warn
8. huge
9. coast
10. steep
11. whole
12. survived

UNDERSTANDING THE MAIN IDEA
Most of the people on Simeulue survived for two reasons: First, the island has hills near the coast. When the tsunami came, people were able to climb the hills. Second, a story warned people to run to the hills after an earthquake.

SCANNING FOR INFORMATION
1. Indonesia
2. Kiro
3. 1907
4. December 26
5. 33
6. on the coast
7. thirty minutes
8. 10 meters
9. fourteen
10. 75,000

CHALLENGE
A.
a. 3
b. 2
c. 2

B.
2 Family saved by their towels
3 Geography lesson saves family
1 Which child to save?

Unit 3

LOOKING AT THE STORY
1. a   4. b   7. a   10. a
2. a   5. b   8. b   11. b
3. a   6. a   9. b   12. a

UNDERSTANDING THE MAIN IDEAS
1. b   2. a   3. b   4. c   5. c   6. b

UNDERSTANDING SUPPORTING DETAILS
1. c   2. e   3. a   4. d   5. b

CHALLENGE
1. c
In Thailand, it is insulting to point your foot at a person.

2. b
In Korea, it is polite for seated passengers on buses to hold the packages of those standing. This is usually done without speaking.

3. b
In France, the customer and the shop owner or salesperson greet one another when the customer enters the shop, and say goodbye when the customer leaves.

4. c
In Nepal, the cost of many things is based on how much the customer can afford to pay. Generally, foreigners are richer than Nepalis, so the shop owner charges you more for the tea than he charges the Nepali man. To the Nepali, it is fair. So, it is best to quietly pay the seven rupees.

5. c
Americans are very busy—so busy that some people don't want to take the time to make friends. To make friends in the United States, you may have to be assertive and take the first step.

6. a
This is all you need to do. Most utility companies in the United States are fair. The first people who call get the first available appointment. (This is called a first-come, first-served basis.)

7. a
In Malaysia, many people are Muslim. Their religion does not permit them to touch a dog or be touched by a dog. (Nonetheless, there are some Muslims who have dogs.)

8. c
It is probably a good idea to turn down the invitation. If the family wanted you to stay for dinner, they would have invited you for dinner.

9. c
The pace of living is slower in Spain than in other countries, and some people do not worry about being on time. Perhaps the best solution is to do what Spaniards do: bring knitting, a book, or a puzzle to pass the time while you wait.

10. c
It is impolite to ask questions about a French person's personal life. (The question that is a conversation-opener in the United States—"What do you do for a living?"—is considered especially impolite in France.) The French would rather talk about politics, history, or the arts.

Unit 4

PRE-READING

All of the statements are false.

LOOKING AT THE STORY

1. a	3. b	5. b	7. a	9. b
2. b	4. a	6. b	8. a	10. a

LOOKING AT SPECIAL EXPRESSIONS

1. c   2. a   3. b

UNDERSTANDING THE MAIN IDEAS

1. c	3. c	5. a	7. c
2. d	4. b	6. c	

UNDERSTANDING SUPPORTING DETAILS

1. d   2. c   3. a   4. b

CHALLENGE

1. a. N   2. a. P   3. a. P
   b. P   b. N   b. N

Unit 5

LOOKING AT THE STORY

1. k	4. c	7. a	10. f
2. i	5. l	8. h	11. b
3. j	6. g	9. e	12. d

UNDERSTANDING THE MAIN IDEAS

1. She was going to study in Paris for a semester.
2. She was 20 years old.
3. He had two photos in his hand.
4. They were his cousin's daughters.
5. The names of the girls were written on the back of the photos.

MAKING INFERENCES

Possible answers:

1. She was excited because
   - she was going to have many new experiences.
   - Paris is a beautiful city.
   - she liked to travel.

   She was nervous because
   - she was going to miss her family.
   - she didn't like to fly.
   - she was afraid she wouldn't understand the French people.
2. She sighed because
   - she didn't want to look for the girls.
   - she thought it would be impossible to find the girls.
   - she thought she wouldn't have time to look for the girls.
3. She
   - ate in restaurants.
   - met a lot of new people.
   - went to museums.
   - shopped.
4. She didn't know there were so many Armenians in Paris.
5. Natalie looked like her father.

6. She
   - went home with her father's cousin.
   - met the cousin's family.
   - called her father to tell him she had met his cousin and her family.

Unit 6

LOOKING AT THE STORY

1. a	4. a	7. b	10. a
2. a	5. a	8. b	11. a
3. a	6. b	9. b	12. b

UNDERSTANDING TIME RELATIONSHIPS

1. 79	3. 79	5. 79	7. 1860	9. 79
2. today	4. 1860	6. 79	8. 79	10. today

UNDERSTANDING CAUSE AND EFFECT

1. c   2. d   3. a   4. e   5. b

CHALLENGE

a. 2   b. 1   c. 4   d. 3   e. 5

Unit 7

LOOKING AT THE STORY

1. a	4. a	7. a	10. b
2. a	5. a	8. b	11. a
3. b	6. a	9. b	12. b

LOOKING AT SPECIAL EXPRESSIONS

1. b	4. d	7. i	10. k	13. o
2. a	5. f	8. h	11. j	14. m
3. c	6. e	9. g	12. l	15. n

UNDERSTANDING CAUSE AND EFFECT

1. b   2. a   3. d   4. e   5. c

UNDERSTANDING DETAILS

1. ~~dollars~~ cents
2. ~~train~~ bus
3. ~~Washington~~ New York
4. ~~driver~~ passenger
5. ~~foot~~ shoulder

CHALLENGE

1. Friday sandwich	fried egg sandwich
2. a lonely child	an only child
3. the best diamond rings	the best onion rings
4. hot socks	hot sauce
5. X-rated	X-rayed
6. self of steam	self-esteem
7. for Richard Stans	for which it stands
8. free eye screening	free ice cream
9. euthanasia	youth in Asia
10. ten issues	tennis shoes

Unit 8

LOOKING AT THE STORY

1. a	5. a	8. a	11. a
2. b	6. b	9. b	12. b
3. a	7. a	10. a	13. a
4. b			

LOOKING AT SPECIAL EXPRESSIONS

1. b	4. d	7. i	10. k
2. a	5. f	8. g	11. j
3. c	6. e	9. h	12. l

UNDERSTANDING CAUSE AND EFFECT

1. c   2. e   3. a   4. d   5. b

UNDERSTANDING DETAILS

1. ~~paint~~ dust   3. ~~new~~ old   5. ~~mathematics~~ geography
2. ~~Rome~~ Paris   4. ~~$30~~ $3

CHALLENGE

Christie's sold the items for these amounts:

Andy Warhol painting	$3.5 million
Lincoln letter	$442,500
Diana's gown	$200,000
Steiff teddy bear	$38,000

Unit 9

LOOKING AT THE STORY

1. b	4. a	7. a	10. b
2. b	5. a	8. b	11. b
3. a	6. a	9. a	12. b

LOOKING AT SPECIAL EXPRESSIONS

1. c	4. e	7. h
2. a	5. f	8. i
3. b	6. d	9. g

UNDERSTANDING THE MAIN IDEAS

Children are usually not superstitious.
It is always a good idea to take a numerologist's advice.
People who use purple towels are silly.

UNDERSTANDING SUPPORTING DETAILS

1. c   2. e   3. d   4. a   5. b

CHALLENGE

a. 7	c. 4	e. 2	g. 5
b. 1	d. 6	f. 3	

Unit 10

LOOKING AT THE STORY

a. 11	d. 2	g. 5	j. 9
b. 6	e. 7	h. 3	k. 1
c. 4	f. 10	i. 8	

LOOKING AT WORDS THAT GO TOGETHER

1. crowd/lion/wind   4. seat
2. bolts   5. landing
3. ice/wet floor   6. hour

FORMING MENTAL IMAGES AS YOU READ

1. ~~A female flight attendant in her mid-twenties is standing at the door of the airplane.~~
2. ~~Another male flight attendant is sitting in the copilot's seat. He is flying the airplane.~~
3. ~~Some of the passengers are screaming and crying.~~
4. ~~The airplane has just landed and is at the end of the runway.~~

UNDERSTANDING SEQUENCE

7:30 Plane takes off.
7:43 Explosion at front of plane; pilot's windshield blows out.
7:46 Copilot calls air-traffic control; asks for emergency landing.
7:49 Air-traffic control tells copilot to land at Southampton airport.
8:02 Passengers leave the plane; paramedics rush in.

DISCUSSION

A. Statistically, the most dangerous part of the trip is the car ride from the man's home to the airport in Chicago.

Unit 11

LOOKING AT THE STORY

1. reminded	6. fool
2. headed	7. evaporates
3. rear bumper	8. detail
4. came to	9. spread by word of
5. realistic	mouth

LOOKING AT SPECIAL EXPRESSIONS

1. b	4. f	7. i
2. a	5. e	8. g
3. c	6. d	9. h

UNDERSTANDING THE MAIN IDEAS

_✔_ a. are not true.
_✔_ c. often take place in or near cities.
_✔_ d. are realistic.
_✔_ e. are friend-of-a-friend stories.
_✔_ f. have many details.
_✔_ h. remain essentially the same, no matter how far they travel.

UNDERSTANDING CAUSE AND EFFECT

1. e   2. d   3. c   4. a   5. b

CHALLENGE

The story about the dog that swallowed the cellular phone (#4) is true. It was reported in five reputable newspapers: the *Washington Post*, the *Boston Herald*, the *Montreal Gazette*, the *Orange County Register*, and the *London Daily Telegraph*. So, the story is (almost certainly) true.

Unit 12

LOOKING AT THE STORY

1. meadow	6. examining
2. surrounding	7. convinced
3. Pirates, treasure	8. investors
4. shovels	9. drills
5. chest	10. enormous

LOOKING AT SPECIAL EXPRESSIONS

1. b   2. a   3. c

UNDERSTANDING TIME RELATIONSHIPS

1. a, b, d   2. a, b, d   3. a, b, c   4. a, c, d   5. a, b, d

SCANNING FOR INFORMATION

1. McGinnis	6. Eight
2. oak	7. evening
3. The next day	8. 1850
4. Two	9. five
5. 13	10. twenty

Unit 13

PRE-READING

The photo was taken in the United States in 1990.

LOOKING AT THE STORY

1. a	4. b	7. b	10. b
2. a	5. b	8. a	11. b
3. a	6. b	9. b	12. a

UNDERSTANDING THE MAIN IDEAS

1. c	2. c	3. a	4. d

UNDERSTANDING SUPPORTING DETAILS

1. c	2. e	3. a	4. d	5. b

CHALLENGE

a. 2	b. 1	c. 3	d. 5	e. 4

Unit 14

LOOKING AT THE STORY

1. f	5. a	8. i	11. j
2. h	6. c	9. b	12. l
3. g	7. m	10. k	13. e
4. d			

UNDERSTANDING A SUMMARY

1. postpone	4. Chinese	7. rose	10. important
2. death	5. Moon	8. same	11. proof
3. rates	6. fell	9. relative	12. facts

SCANNING FOR INFORMATION

1. 86	7. Israel
2. two	8. Thomas
3. California	9. Declaration of Independence
4. Passover	10. 1776
5. two	11. fifty
6. Connecticut	12. days

Unit 15

LOOKING AT THE STORY

1. eager	8. impatient
2. gathered	9. the least of their worries
3. attract	10. announced
4. supplies	11. amazement
5. frowned	12. arrested
6. cautious	13. sentence
7. greeted	14. consulted

LOOKING AT SPECIAL EXPRESSIONS

1. c	3. a	5. d
2. b	4. f	6. e

UNDERSTANDING THE MAIN IDEAS

1. c	3. c	5. c	7. a
2. a	4. a	6. b	

SCANNING FOR INFORMATION

1. 1950	6. suitcase
2. newspaper	7. noon
3. F.	8. mayor
4. 24	9. Missouri
5. two	10. phoned

CHALLENGE

All five "opportunities" are scams. This is how each scam works:

1. When people send in their $37 deposit, they do not get envelopes and sales brochures. They might get instructions on how to place ads like the one they responded to, so that they can cheat other people out of their money. (So, they will be stuffing envelopes, but not for a legitimate business.) Or they might get a list of companies that are supposedly interested in having people stuff envelopes.

2. This is probably a trick. The models who are "selected" by the modeling agency will be asked to sign a contract agreeing to pay several hundred dollars for professional photographs. Sometimes the modeling agency never distributes the photos to businesses, and sometimes the agency never even gives the potential models their photos. The company simply packs up and leaves town.

3. This ad guarantees that "we will match you with a scholarship." That only means they will give you information about a possible scholarship; it doesn't mean that you will actually get the scholarship. Scholarship information is available free from most U.S. universities and high schools.

4. This offer is for a 1:39 scale-model car. That means that for your $21.99, you will get a model car that is one-thirty-ninth the size of a real car. (And they are keeping these little cars, probably made of plastic, in a "secured facility"!)

5. This is a classic chain letter. The idea that everyone who participates in a chain letter will make money is mathematically impossible. This particular chain letter asks you to send the letter on to 100 people. Each of those 100 people would then send the letter on to 100 more people. Each of those 10,000 people would send the letter on to 100 more people. If everyone who received a letter sent it on to 100 people, by the fifth mailing, ten billion people would receive the letter. That's more than twice the population of the world! The very first investors in the chain might receive money, but later investors rarely get back their original investments ($25 for the five people on the list, plus the cost of copying and mailing the letter). Also, this type of chain letter is illegal in the United States.

Unit 16

LOOKING AT THE STORY

1. laundry
2. engaged
3. grief
4. thoughts kept returning
5. trained
6. track suit
7. occasionally
8. stunned
9. admires
10. cheered
11. refugee
12. no strings attached

UNDERSTANDING CAUSE AND EFFECT

1. d 2. b 3. e 4. a 5. c

UNDERSTANDING SUPPORTING DETAILS

1. b 2. a 3. c 4. e 5. d

DISCUSSION

B. Mirsada Buric-Adam's graduated from the university with a degree in journalism. She no longer runs competitively; she is a newspaper reporter now. In fact, if you search "Mirsada Buric" on the Internet, you will find not only articles about Mirsada but articles by Mirsada. She writes in English for Arizona newspapers and lives in Arizona with Eric and their daughter.

CHALLENGE

1. Keino got out of the taxi and ran the 2 kilometers to the stadium. So, while his competitors were resting and preparing themselves mentally for the race, he was jogging through the crowded streets of Mexico City. He arrived at the stadium minutes before the race. He won the 1,500, setting a world record. After the Olympics, he had surgery for an infected gall bladder.

2. Vera continued to practice while living in the village. She kept in shape by swinging from tree branches and practiced her floor exercises in a meadow. In the end, the government allowed her to compete in Mexico City, where she won two gold medals and two silvers. She was a favorite of the crowd, especially after she married fellow Olympian Josef Odiozil in Mexico City.

3. Redmond's father, Jim, was watching the race from the stands. He ran down to the track and, paying no attention to the security guards who tried to stop him, rushed to his son. Derek put his arm around his father. Holding his father's hand and sobbing, Redmond limped toward the finish line. A few feet from the finish line, Redmond let go of his father and finished the race on his own. The crowd of 65,000 gave him a standing ovation.

Reference Map

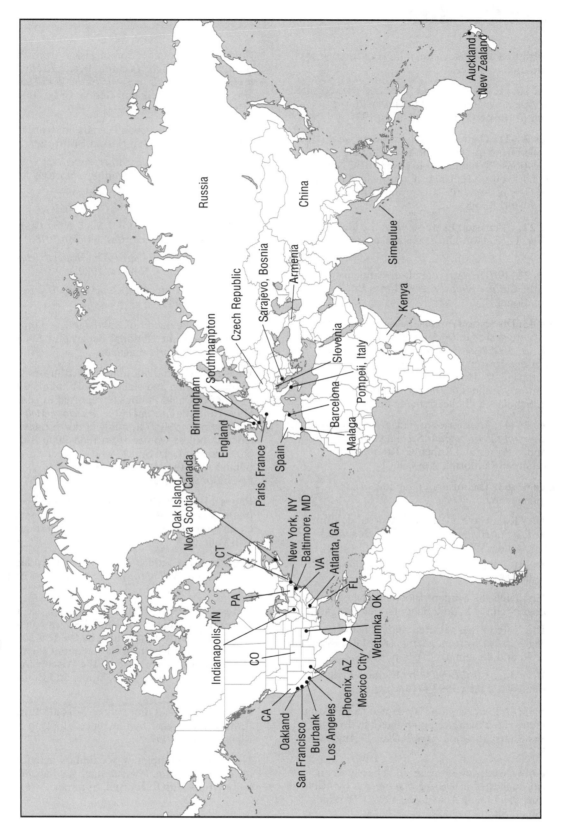

Text Credits

We wish to acknowledge the following sources of information and ideas:

Pages 10–11: "Flowers" and "Peanuts" are reprinted from *True Love: Stories Told to and by Robert Fulghum*, HarperCollins Publishers, 1997.

Pages 20–21: The first-person accounts were compiled from quotations in the following publications: "Which child to save?" BBC News, 12/31/04; CTV.ca, 12/31/04; "Family saved by their towels" *People*, 1/17/05; "Geography lesson saves family" *Sun*, 1/1/05

Page 27: Discussion Exercise 4A is the idea of Jean Stocker, TESL-L on-line discussion group, 7 April 1999.

Pages 28–29: The quiz on cultures and customs is from the *Culture Shock!* series. Times Books International.

Page 43: Discussion exercise 4A is based on an activity suggested in *Once Upon a Time: Using Stories in the Classroom* by Mario Rinvolucri, Cambridge University Press, 1983. ("Time-travel mirror, page 92) He in turn credits S. Striker and E. Kimmer, authors of *The Second Anti-Colouring Book*, Scholastic Publications, London, 1980.

Pages 46–47: The stories are adapted from *Legacies: The Story of the Immigrant Second Generation* by Alejandro Portes and Ruben G. Rumbaut, University of California Press, 2001.

Pages 62–63: The misunderstandings were compiled from:

▸ The "Kids Have a Way with Words" column in *Taste of Home* magazine, P.O. Box 992, Greendale, WI 53129 (#1 and #4);

▸ The Web site of Medical Transcriptionists Daily (#5);

▸ Mrs. Nielsen's Student Bloopers page, Mount Logan (Utah) Middle School's Web site (#6);

▸ The "Life in these United States" feature of *Reader's Digest* magazine, (#3 May 1999, p. 76 and #8 January 1999, p. 80);

▸ *More Anguished English* by Richard Lederer, Delacorte Press, 1993 (#10).

Page 65: "A Real Bargain" is adapted from "Paris map may show man route to riches," by Jo Ellen Meyers Sharp, the *Indianapolis Star*, 17 August 1985.

Page 68: Discussion exercise 4B is based on an activity suggested in *Writing Inspirations* by Arlene Marcus, Pro Lingua Associates, 1996. ("Bargaining in a Small Shop," page 24)

Page 87: The information on risk is from *Risk: A Practical Guide for Deciding What's Really Safe and What's Really Dangerous in the World Around You* by David Ropeik and George Gray, Houghton Mifflin Company, 2002.

Pages 88–95: The urban legends are from the following books by Jan Harold Brunvand:

▸ *The Vanishing Hitchhiker: American Urban Legends and Their Meanings*. Norton, 1981.

▸ *The Choking Doberman and Other "New" Urban Legends*. Norton, 1984.

▸ *The Mexican Pet: More "New" Urban Legends and Some Old Favorites*. Norton, 1986.

▸ *Curses! Broiled Again!: The Hottest Urban Legends Going*. Norton, 1989.

▸ *The Baby Train: And Other Lusty Urban Legends*. Norton, 1993.

Page 97: "The Secret of Oak Island," adaptation by permission of the National Geographic Society, © June 1989, *World* magazine

Page 113: The statistics on the death rates of elderly Chinese women and elderly Jewish men are the findings of David Phillips as reported in *Lancet* (1988) and the *Journal of the American Medical Association* (1990). The study of death rates of elderly Chinese women from 1985–2000 is the work of economist Gary Smith, whose research was published in the May/June 2004 issue of *Psychosomatic Medicine*.

Pages 118–119: The "cutting the lemon" guided imagery is suggested by Dr. Martin L. Rossman, co-director of the Academy for Guided Imagery in Mill Valley, CA.

Page 119: The guided imagery script is adapted from *Staying Well with Guided Imagery* by Belleruth Naparstek, Warner Books, 1994.

Pages 128–129: The "dishonest tricks" are actual scams that people in the United States received in the mail. They were provided by the U.S. Postal Inspection Service. Information about the way the scams work was provided by the Wisconsin Department of Agriculture, Trade, and Consumer Protection.

Page 131: To read more about Mirsada Buric, see "Love Under Siege" by Lawrence Elliott in *Reader's Digest*, March 1997.

The sentence completion vocabulary activity is the idea of Sally Winn. ("Vocabulary Revitalized" by Sally Winn, TESOL Journal, Summer 1996)

Photo Credits

Page 2: Corbis

Page 10: Mike Zens/Corbis

Page 11: Envision/Corbis

Page 12: Ed Wray/AP/Wide World Photos

Page 21: *(a)* NI Syndication, *(b)* Empics, *(c)* West Australian

Page 22: Courtesy of Friendship Force International

Page 30: Lou Mack/Los Angeles Times

Page 38: Courtesy of Natalie Garibian Peters

Page 48: Lou Battaglia/National Geographic Society

Page 55: *(a,b)* Mimmo Jodice/Corbis, *(c)* Werner Forman/Art Resource, NY, *(d)* Farrell Grehan/Corbis, *(e)* Gian Berto Vanni/Corbis

Page 56: Sandra Heyer

Page 64: Rick Myers

Page 70: Christie's Images

Page 71: *(top)* Christie's Images, *(bottom)* Archive Photos

Page 72: Sandra Heyer

Page 80: Empics

Page 86: Stephen Carr

Page 88: Corbis/Bettmann

Page 96: Corbis/Bettmann

Page 104: Courtesy of the Pennsylvania Dutch Visitors Bureau

Page 111: *(a)* Bob Rowan/Corbis, *(b)* © Mel Horst, Witmer, PA, *(c,d)* Courtesy of Pennsylvania Dutch Visitors Bureau, *(e)* © Mel Horst, Witmer, PA

Page 112: Corbis/Bettman

Page 120: Courtesy of the Hughes County Times

Page 128: Vince Streano/Corbis

Page 130: AP/Wide World Photos

Page 136: *(top)* Getty Images, *(bottom)* Tony Duffy/Getty Images

Page 137: Gray Mortimore/Getty Images

Acknowledgments

I wish to thank:

- The many teachers who have written me or sought me out at TESOL conventions to tell me about their experiences with the True Stories books. Your feedback helps me assess how the stories and exercises are working outside the small sphere of my own classroom. Your suggestions are always welcome.

- Peggy Miles for field-testing stories and exercises at the Santa Cruz Adult School, Santa Cruz, CA;

- Students at the Santa Cruz Adult School, Santa Cruz, CA; the American Language Institute, IUP; the University of Wisconsin, Whitewater; and Whitewater Community Education, Whitewater, WI, for the examples for the writing exercises. In particular, I wish to thank student authors Carmen Valverde Diaz, Yoshiko Araki, Yukari Fukutani, Aldo Motta, Ines Brandes, and Marcela Ayale for their contributions to this third edition;

- Karen Davy for the expert editorial help;

- Laura Le Dréan for being the first reader of all the new stories;

- Wendy Campbell for help with the photos;

- Françoise Leffler for the eleventh-hour editorial suggestions;

- Danielle Belfiore for skillfully guiding the book through its final stages;

- Lynn Edwards, who facilitated obtaining permission to reprint from Robert Fulghum's book;

- E. David Luria, Patrice Reynolds, Gloria Greenbaum, Trudy Janke, Joe Parris, Kathy Dodson, Charles Cook, and many other members of Friendship Force International for sharing anecdotes, photos, and clippings;

- Anna Hughes Carone for the information about the stages of culture shock;

- Narrye Caldwell for information about acupuncture and alternative types of medicine;

- Natalie Garibian Peters for graciously helping with "If You Have Time";

- Jeff Korman at the Enoch Pratt Free Library, Baltimore, for information about the *bum/bomb* mixup;

- Cyrus Rowshan and Sharron Bassano for their accounts of "misunderstandings";

- John Shaughnessy at the *Indianapolis Star* for information about the map;

- Christina Geiger at Christie's for providing a copy of Christie's Year in Review, 1997;

- Mindy Geller at the Toyota Corporation for verifying the Toyoda/Toyota story;

- Ali Aghbar, Ray Thomas, and Geraldine Zalazar at IUP for relinquishing class time so that I could question their students about superstitions;

- Nancy and Annamarie Pontier for telling me about Flight 5390;

- Huisen Shi and Rong Liu for their descriptions of the Harvest Moon Festival and Don Eisen for his description of Passover;

- Glen Loyd, Wisconsin Department of Agriculture, Trade and Consumer Protection and Lori Groen of the U.S. Postal Inspection Service for providing information about scams and actual examples of schemes;

- Mirsada Buric for graciously helping with "Love Under Siege."